You are Enough for Him

By Emree Webb

Disclaimer: I have fallen into the trap far too many times of the mindset that if a book is not of my faith, I cannot read it. I seek to share my story, and with that comes my religion. This book is not written to change the church you attend. I write to allow Christ to change your heart and your mind. I cannot deny what I know, just as I would never inhibit someone else from sharing theirs. Throughout the book, I will list various scriptures and study methods unique to my faith, as well as others I discovered from people whose beliefs are different from mine. In a world so divided and confused, why should we not be the first to mend the rift? Feel free to study whatever scriptures may be pertinent to you, but if you are interested in learning more, I have included verses from the Book of Mormon. Thank you for supporting the message of hope and the eradication of fear.

I've always wanted to write a book.

Strange desire for someone who hasn't even turned 21 years old, right?

This is a story about the experiences I've had in the short years of my life. I'm young. I'm an amateur. I don't claim to be a psychologist or a medical doctor. I'm unremarkable in so many ways. But those are so often the ones whom God most chooses to work with. (Ether 12:27, 2 Corinthians 12:7-10, 2 Nephi 3:21) The idea to publish this book began because I wanted to prove to myself that I could do it, that I could have the perseverance to finish something so famously difficult to achieve. However, with time, this manuscript transformed into a beam of light for me. Writing this book allowed me to see my Savior, not physically, but spiritually. I know Him. And He knows me, just as He knows you. (Psalm 147:3-4)

2 Nephi 26:33 says, "For [God] doeth that which is good among the children of men; and he doeth nothing save it be plain unto the children of men; and he inviteth them all to come unto him and partake of his goodness; and he denieth none that come unto him, black and white, bond and free, male and female; and he remembereth the heathen; and all are alike unto God."

This book is written for those of you whose lives have been dominated by fear. Choking, gripping, air-swallowing terror controls every step of your existence. This book is for people with anxiety, toxic perfectionism, eating disorders, depression, and just plain worry that life isn't going to work out in their favor. Maybe you think you don't fall into any of those categories. Maybe your situation isn't soul-engulfing or spirit-shaking. Maybe you're just a mom who worries about her teenage children or a recently jobless college student wondering how you're going to make ends meet.

THAT IS FEAR. What I'm offering you is a chance to escape. Maybe where you're at right now doesn't seem so bad. Heck, you're successful! You've got awards and achievements piled up in every direction, but let me share with you a secret I learned and am currently still learning: you will never be happy if you continue to push toward perfection NOW. Your mental health is important. You are IMPORTANT.

I don't offer studies in this book or medical advice; I am simply offering my story of how I escaped. And even better than that, I am offering you a chance to do the same through the Master of the Tempest (Matthew 8:26).

Our Savior has provided an escape, and I wish to allow every man, woman, and child the opportunity to grasp it. This book is for you, regardless of your circumstances. _Do not give up hope._

Fear will always be present in our lives and predominant in mental health. It is the constant, immobilizing apprehension that we will someday park our car outside those pearly gates, weighed down by regret. In a way, everyone is on some part of the fear spectrum because we all have fears.

Period.

From the time you were little to the day you lay down in your grave, fears will penetrate your carefully constructed shell, and you will have two choices: bend to them or make them bend to you.

Where does that strength come from? Jesus Christ said in Revelation 1:17-18, "And He laid his right hand upon me, saying unto me, Fear not, I am the first and the last: I _am_ he that liveth, and was dead; and, behold, I am alive forevermore, Amen, and have the keys of hell and of death."

Jesus Christ is the key. He has all keys, all rights, and all power (Matthew 16:19). Your happiness depends on Him, but it also depends on you. Fear has a way of making itself the driver. You have keys, lots of them, because your Father in Heaven loves you. But when you climb into that car, you may be surprised to see fear sitting in the driver's seat beside you. He starts as a backseat driver, nagging here and there, reminding you of stoplights, stop signs, and pedestrians. But each time you drive, fear points out more and more things. Your anxiety grows. Don't hit the chipmunk. Watch out for the speed bump. Cop car! Cop car! Slow down, you're going 1 mph over.

Before long, you start handing over the keys to Fear. He drives your car to places you really didn't want to go. You are scared now, which is exactly what Fear intended for you in the first place. You may have noticed Fear now has a capital F. Not a typo. Fear is real. He has a name, and it is Satan. If you don't learn to teach fear how to keep its big mouth shut, then you will lose control of your life. You will drive off the path you intended to reach. How do I know? Because that is exactly what Fear did to me.

When you couple Jesus Christ with the teachings from this book, you will leave no room for Fear in the front seat because our Savior will have taken His place (2 Timothy 1:7). Fear will still ride in the car occasionally, but he won't have nearly the influence that he did before. You will see your own value, your own self-worth, and you will see how proud the Messiah and our Heavenly Father truly are of you.

I invite you to come and see, come and change, come and grow. You may be surprised by what God has in store for you. (Luke 18:16-17)

Types of Fear: *Note: This is not a comprehensive nor all-inclusive list, but simply a few examples. Remember that everyone is different, and your feelings are valid and worth noting down. I invite you, as you read through this book, to look for signs of fear in yourself.*

- Toxic perfectionism: fear of failure

- Chronic stress: fear of not being able to handle everything

- Diagnosed anxiety: fear of the past and the future

- Clinical depression: fear of oneself, fear of dying alone

- OCD: fear of never being able to control oneself

- Low Self Esteem: fear that no one will ever love you
- PTSD: fear that you are too broken to be useful
- Social anxiety: fear of rejection from your peers
- Scrupulosity: fear of failing before God
- Bulimia or Anorexia: fear of getting fat
- Bipolar disorder: fear of feeling nothing and never getting what you need to feel joy

TABLE OF CONTENTS

CHAPTER 1: ROOTS

Ronald A Rasband said, "Fear is not new. The disciples of Jesus Christ, out on the Sea of Galilee, feared the 'windand the waves' in the dark of the night. As His disciples today, we, too, have fears. Our single adults fear making commitments such as getting married. Young marrieds, like our children, can fear bringing children into an increasingly wicked world. Missionaries fear lots of things, especially approaching strangers. Widows fear going forward alone. Teenagers fear not being accepted, grade schoolers fear the first day of school, and university students fear getting back a test. We fear failure, rejection, disappointment, and the unknown. We fear hurricanes, earthquakes, and fires that ravage the land and our lives. We fear not being chosen, and on the flip side, we fear being chosen. We fear not being good enough; we fear that the Lord has no blessings for us. We fear change, and our fears can escalate to terror. Have I included just about everyone?"

We believe in being honest

Far too often, we only allow people to see a hollow shell, an exterior seven layers thick that protects us from their compassion (Proverbs 14:13). And what is sealed on the inside? Well, we are. We walk down 47 flights of stairs, twist the combinations in the dim, flickering light, and shut the door to the outside world. Everyone holds a different form of a secret. Secrets come and go in life. It is not the secret that tips us over the edge but the emotional burden attached to keeping it.

Hatred, anxiety, and unrest bubble up like a coke sitting in the hot sun. In a moment, it fizzles out and loses all feeling together. In our hearts, we know that we shouldn't be feeling this way, but that only makes it worse. Our society has impressed upon us for so long the need to brush fear away like a moth fluttering toward the light. It was necessary for survival in generations before to hide your despair. Children needed to be fed. Work needed to be done. Survival. That's what it has always been about. But that isn't what Christ is all about. He wants you to do more than barely scrape by.

It is not weakness to admit you are weak (Isaiah 35:3-4). You are stronger than your fellow man when, from the depths of your shallow reserves, you slide into your true state.

You cannot hide from yourself. Fear will try to warp you, casting creeping shadows over your mind. I have these thoughts that no one hears. Fear binds my arms and feet with ropes, chains, and weights that drag me down to the murky depths of a silty sea bottom. I can't share them. I'm too afraid. We fear the judgment of others whose lives seem to be untouched by the strain of mental health. We fear being viewed as debilitated or unlovable. Our neighbors and friends don't struggle like we do! If you were able to see within every American household, you might find yourself surprised.

A life that appears ideal is not real. More often than not, the people who find the most success are the ones who struggle the most. Grief and suffering must be observed and felt in order to eradicate it (Matthew 5:4, 3 Nephi 12:4). You're keeping yourself safe from exactly what you need: relief. That's exactly what fear wants for you – to feel oddly secure in your own self-demolition.

You do not need to protect the world from you. You are an incredible creation of your Heavenly Father (Psalm 95:7). He created you to champion in this life. These tendencies that you may have can be formidable at times. They are malignant tumors that grow and spread, eating up your well-being. Even if you feel like the vast majority of the time, you are able to control your thoughts, which may tie into the problem further down the road. You see, suppressed emotions turn into a shell, which turns into a maze that we someday must learn how to navigate and escape.

Our unconscious brains are powerful. Your subconscious can filter 11 million thoughts per second, but only 40-50 bits of information stay in your memory.[1]

The more we push a thought away, the more it flips to return. This is called the "rebound effect."

"You can deplete your mental resources by trying to suppress a thought repeatedly or for a long time, meaning you will eventually be unsuccessful. You may also have trouble suppressing thoughts if your mental resources are already depleted, like when you're feeling stressed, tired, or distracted by something else." -Owen Kelly, PhD [2]

One of the most common feelings we suppress is self-hatred. It is so easy to say unkind things to ourselves. No one can hear us, after all. But our parents taught us what bullying is, so we shove the horrible insults down, trying to stay positive. Over time, this endless cycle develops into almost another persona, a vicious voice in our head that is relentless in tearing us down.

The Bully in My Brain.

I call him "Big Meanie." He pounds his big fists against the interior of my skull, drumming out a senseless melody that weakens my resolve to move forward, one blow at a time. Big Meanie is a minion of fear, a brute henchman who steals my lunch money and shoves my head in the toilet until my ears are swamped in putrid water. I don't remember when I invited him into my house; I imagined he entered without my permission. I start every day at the table with Big Meanie, eating my Cheerios and listening to him rant on and on about how revolting I am. Everything I do circles back to the same process: fail, flounder, rewind.

Doctrine and Covenants 93:24-25 says, "And truth is a knowledge of things as they are and as they were and as they are to come. And whatsoever is more or less than this is the spirit of that wicked one who was a liar from the beginning."

Fear is a liar. Big Meanie is a liar. They will say anything they possibly can to throw you off balance – those incessant thoughts of inadequacy that you push away. When you are weak, those thoughts fly in a fury around your mind, causing you to question if maybe they are right.

I'll never be good enough.

I hate myself.

I don't think I can do this.

I have to keep working so I can reach my goal. I'll never be satisfied until I do.

I can't stop until [*insert something*] is complete.

I'm going to double-check and triple-check and maybe even quadruple-check.

Terrifying? Yes. Unstoppable? No. Big Meanie works for Fear. Fear is the CEO of Satan. In the plan of our Heavenly Father, evil will never win. He created you to be able to beat your own negative thoughts. So, where do you begin?

It starts with allowing your thoughts to coexist peacefully. To enter in and out of your consciousness on a highway of self understanding. It reminds me of a university atmosphere, one of constant change and renewal.

Letting the thoughts come and go as they please…

When I was a young, unmarried college student, I lived with several different groups of roommates. Now, every dynamic of an apartment is different, and I saw that semester after semester, but one trend remained consistent evidently. People come and go. Sometimes, they would enter in droves, one roommate's friend filling the living room and taking up all the space on the couch. Other times, it might be one or two of them with their boyfriends sizzling something in a pan in the kitchen while the others chatted and scrolled through Instagram. It wasn't always easy to share the already small space with so many different personalities. There were disagreements at times, as well as betrayals and hurt feelings. But there was also so much fun: slumber parties, late-night talks, and breakup ice cream runs. These memories pop into my consciousness like fireworks, bright and brilliant, then fade out to make way for the next explosion.

I only have one roommate now: my cute husband. Even now, as we remain together, I know this is a time I will come to cherish someday. Not for its perfection or lack of disappointment but for its rarity. I used to cling to old habits, old thoughts, and old rituals that seemed so second nature to me. They were like pairs of stained pants that I was always embarrassed to wear but still refused to throw away because of their sentimental value.

Your thoughts will also come and go in your life. Sometimes, they will be loud. You will wish they would leave you alone in peace to focus on your homework. Sometimes, they will be sad, and you will long for solace. There will be unkind thoughts from our favorite "Big Meanie" that will make you feel inferior. It is an art to learn to let them go. Resist the urge to tense up and clench harder to the thought. Don't push it away. Simply let them be. And remember these simple three truths:

1) I am a child of God.

2) I know that somehow, someway, it will be ok if I trust in Him

3) Jesus Christ is my Savior, and he can save me

WHEN I CAN'T FEEL THE SPIRIT

Oftentimes, when I allow the thoughts of my divine identity to permeate my tornado of anxiety, I feel at rest. Big Meanie's voice remains quiet for a while, and I feel happy. But sometimes I don't. There are times when I feel so hopelessly unnoticed or so utterly overwhelmed that I can't feel anything. I can't feel God's love, because the panic is so concentrated.

Maybe you've had similar thoughts:

Does God actually care?

Why am I struggling so much if God really is concerned about me?

Is He listening?

Why is this happening to me?

Am I unworthy?

"Yea, behold, I will tell you in your mind and in your heart, by the Holy Ghost, which shall come upon you and which shall dwell in your heart." -Doctrine and Covenants 8:4-2

Have you ever tasted flour and water mixed together before? I have. You can add more flour or pour more water, but no matter what you do, the taste is insipid. Tasteless. Flavorless. Life can be like that sometimes.

Hundreds of people pass you by in the week. Their protruding stomachs, stylish new bangs, or sleek hot rods don't even catch your eye because all you taste is the bland mixture of flour and water. Colors fade to black and white, dimming even the glow of the sun or the warble of a sparrow. The sidewalk is dusty again, which you notice as you stare at your feet, trying not to let anyone discern how muddy your thoughts are.

Somehow, the idea of sharing the gray, churning waste inside your brain only makes the torture sink into complete abandon. To let someone else process the midnight of your mind only seems unjust. Why should you cause others to suffer? Or why expose your own weakness?

No, it is better to do it alone. So you do. Meaningless mornings blend into damp nights, where you writhe under your own thoughts. Heavy. Tepid. Bleak.

Vivek Murphy, a US General Surgeon, once said, "We know that loneliness is a common feeling that many people experience. It's like hunger or thirst. It's a feeling the body sends us when something we need for survival is missing."

It's like young children banging together pots and pans that contain nothing of substance. Only noise and confusion.

And the worst part is that you don't really know how to escape the lonely lack of emotion. It is a black hole that swallows your universe one planet at a time. Isn't the Holy Ghost supposed to be our comforter? Isn't He supposed to be with us at all times? If God truly loved us, why would He leave us in our greatest moments of distress?

I find that walking alone is quite tasteless. I have often found comfort in the words of Romans Chapter 5, which reads:

"Therefore being justified by faith, we have peace with God through our Lord Jesus Christ:

By whom also we have access by faith into this grace wherein we stand and rejoice in the hope of the glory of God.

And not only *so,* but *we glory in tribulations* also: knowing that tribulation worketh patience;

And patience, experience; and experience, hope: And hope maketh not ashamed; because the love of God is shed abroad in our hearts by the Holy Ghost which is given unto us."

To be clear, no one is minimizing your pain here. There is nothing more devastating than that aching hunger for God's love. But wandering that withering path on your own will only deepen the gnawing desire to feel something more. It's time to forgo the solitude of your own mind. It's time to find someone to trust.

STEP ONE: Find Your Safety Buddy

He was the only one who saw me. The day I met Nathan Webb, I told myself it would probably never work out between us. I licked peanut butter off my fingers as we whipped up a batch of cookies for our first date. I liked him. But I didn't like me.

As time progressed, so did the feelings. I had spent my entire life being strong, brave, independent, and smiling through the storm. My smile was my signature calling card. Almost no one could read me through my 32 pearly whites except Nathan.

He saw right past my facade the first time I nearly had a panic attack, though I didn't know that's what it was at the time. My smile wobbled, and tears began to fall. I was too embarrassed for words to describe. But I couldn't hide it from him. Not then, nor now.

I had to learn to trust him, to love him, even when I struggled to feel anything for myself. I felt like a failure, and over time, I couldn't keep it away from Nathan.

The first time I told him the depth of my despair, it was a mixture of relief and destruction. He was lifting away my armor, and I both loved and hated the effect.

1) I felt weak

2) I felt loved

3) I felt needed

The weakness nearly buckled me. I cried for nearly three hours, clutching his arms and wiping away snot dribbling down my nose. He cried with me. We both felt the weight of the sadness sometimes. Nathan became my best friend. Then, my husband. Now, he is my safety.

You cannot do this alone.

You should not do this alone.

Ponder this: Are you being honest with the people you love the most? Are you hiding from them how you truly feel? How can you include them more in your remedial journey? If you find it difficult to share with others (like I did), who is one person you think you can trust with your heart?

YOUR RELATIONSHIP WITH JESUS CHRIST…

Before I knew how to share my pain with people I knew, I often repeated this phrase to myself, "I'm here, and I'm writing. Sometimes I'm not sure why."

It brings me back to a sunrise morning in Hawaii…

Curling my toes in the sand, I observe a tiny crab scurry over my foot as a salty sea breeze teases my hair, exposing my sunburned neck. It's morning now, and I inhale the aroma of change. A soft wave laps the tips of my feet, gently summoning the sand to return with it. I take another step into the water. Nobody is on our beach yet, and I find a haven there.

Here, I am safe from homework, deadlines, and work. But I am not safe from myself. I suppose that is why I'm writing this book. I'm on a hiatus from something icily indifferent to all love. It's like the ocean in the midst of a storm, mammoth fists smashing fishing boats to pieces, swallowing them up in the murky depth. Though the sea is secure, it is also savage. I am the ocean. Vast in span and endless in depth. Will I ever accept all of it? Both the Arctic ice and the Mexican reefs are part of the same ocean. It houses trillions of lifeforms and provides a living for thousands. Yet if you find yourself in the midst of the tempest… lookout.

Jesus did not sink in the sea (Matthew 25:25-32). He walked on top of it, even in the hurricane. Though others nearly drowned, he would not allow them to do so if they merely extended their hand.

I suppose you are looking for a solution to all your problems. Me too.

I found it. It is him. All fear, all anxiety, all dread stops with him. I can't explain it, but it is to be caught in his net and scooped up into his arms. If I didn't want him, he would carefully let me swim back into the sea, but I am not a fish. I am not insignificant. Where I see endless commotion and disaster, my Savior sees new life growing within me. I am the endless sea of possibilities.

And you are, too.

It's time to reach up.

Start with prayer.

It's okay. Take my word.

Let me take you on a walk with God…

My conversation with God:

God: Do you see what I see now?

Me: I'm trying.

God: You are enough. You are my daughter.

Me: I hear you, Lord. I trust you. My fears are not as big as you.

God: Give them to me. Your fears matter. You matter. I love you. Don't give up hope yet. Walk a little further. The sun is on the horizon. The darkness will end. I am waiting for you.

Me: God, I will continue. I am walking towards you. Make my paths straight and sure because I often feel lost in my journey.

God: All I ask is that you walk. Direction, my daughter. Walk in the right direction.

This book is going to list many different thinking patterns associated with anxiety, OCD, toxic perfectionism, depression, and many other mental illnesses. The goal is not for you to self-diagnose yourself and announce over the Walmart intercom that you have x,y,z problems. If you notice one or more of these thinking patterns in your life, I invite you to follow the pattern of this book, one step at a time. Don't obsess over whether you are or aren't broken. You are; trust me, we all are a little broken. Don't worry about what other people will think of you. This is a journey between you and God. A journey of becoming and overcoming. You and your thoughts are safe here.[3]

Now, I'm not suggesting that if you grapple with your trepidation, you are now diagnosed with a mental health disorder. However, I am suggesting that one of the easiest ways to begin to lose interest in life is to suppress our feelings, any of them!

Think of the movie *Inside Out.* The main character, Riley, and all of the people around her have five basic emotions in their brains: anger, disgust, fear, joy, and sadness. Each of those main emotions is represented by a tiny human who controls much of the motherboard of this subject's actions. However, at the commencement of the movie, Riley's life is generally dominated by one emotion: Joy. She mostly controls Riley's life, while Riley's other emotions are pushed off to the side. Inside Riley's intelligence also lies her core memories, the things that have shaped Riley into the person she is. All of those recollections are joyful until one day when a core memory comes that is downcast instead of fun-filled. Upon moving to a new city with new people, Riley truly experiences what it is to be alone. In the end, Riley discovers that it is ok to feel a mixture of emotions; in fact, this is part of life – to feel, to experience, and to know.

MY ROOTS

Maybe fear, true fear, cannot be eradicated because it is not meant to be in the grand scheme of God's plan. Perhaps that counterfeit knockoff fear that Satan pours into our hands needs to be carved and reconstructed. Perhaps this is the great test of life – not to destroy as Satan does, but to create like our Savior Jesus Christ. When the great Jehovah says, "Fear not what man can do; for perfect love casteth out all fear." (Moroni 8:16) Countless times, we are told not only to "fear not" but also to trust God. (Doctrine and Covenants 38:30, Doctrine and Covenants 68:6, Genesis 26:24, Isa. 51:7, Alma 56:46–48). Instead of wiping out fear, God solely intends us to mold it and transfer it.

I spent 21 years of my life denying the undeniable. Not that I didn't recognise my own unhappiness. It seeped into my relationship with my husband. It soaked into the spaghetti I made for dinner, the pencil I scraped through homework assignments, and the basketball as it bounced into the hoop. Fear leaks into every aspect of your life.

I could be classified as a workaholic. I make goals, set them, and achieve them. From the time I was young, my self-constructed castle of excellence loomed over me, pushing me daily to see how far I could stretch my limits. In my mind, if I was not moving towards a goal, I was tumbling backward, and I needed to keep advancing. There were different pivotal moments in my life. When I was in high school, I poured my soul into track, FFA, yearbook, basketball, cross country, student government, 4H, church callings, and almost any other way I could keep myself busy. If someone needed a hand, the answer was indefinitely yes, no matter how many things teetered precariously on my plate. I strove for excellence, which in my mind were medals, trophies, and acknowledgment from the people around me.

This phrase pelleted my mind unceasingly, "You can give a little more. Keep going."

Until I reached the point of exhaustion. Always. Wilting on my scratchy carpet and begging for my mind to take the foot off the gas. This has always been a theme for me. Give until you have no more to give. Drain the resources until you become a wrinkly, disgusting raisin. Walk until you can walk no further until ice climbs your veins and your temperature drops into a lifetime of endless winter. I know some of you can relate to me. For the longest time, I braved the unbearable loneliness, wondering if anyone else could be as frightened as I was. It was my duty to carry the world on my shoulders, and that attitude drove me to greatness… though I could never see it.

It became an obsession, a quest, an accomplishment. I never saw myself as succeeding. I looked at myself in the mirror every morning and told myself, "You can be a little better today! Yesterday was good, but today must be better." I felt so worried about success. It came to the point that I had panic attacks every time I fell short of what I wanted to accomplish. My life became a monotonous to-do list. I took for granted the strength God had given me. Then I met Turian.

My Friend Who Taught Me to Live

Turian Carrion suffered from crippling Rheumatoid arthritis. She lived in the back alleys on a dangerous street lined with thugs and punks poking around for money. But we loved to visit her. We would pay the taxi fees and squeal up to Turian's front door to enter and see those fine paintings hung on her pristinely white walls. She always brought out the biggest plate of cookies I had ever seen, all while recounting her days as a school teacher before her slim hands became twisted and gnarled by self-destructive immunogenic cells.

Her gray eyes always fascinated me the most. Though all her children had somewhat fallen away from the church, those eyes retained a brightness like the swords of the people of Ammon. Turian Carrion could not even roll out of bed by herself, yet every week, she arranged for someone to pick her up and bring her to church. Tithing was paid promptly at the end of each week, though she did not work. One day, as we visited our dear friend, she hefted a curled hand on top of mine.

"I've been practicing that," she said with a wink.

"Hermana Turian," I finally asked, "How do you do it? What keeps you going? You sit day after day in that chair, yet you are so happy!"

Turian smiled a gray old smile of someone who lived a life of more pain than just her disease, "It began to hurt when I was about

30 years old," she began. "A searing bluntness that throbbed in my legs even going up the steps to the bus. But I continued onward. They diagnosed me with arthritis and told me what my fate would be. I was determined to overcome it, to become the first to fight past the damage my own body was inflicting. It was no use. I saw, with the passing of time, my bones warp and swell. For a while, I was in such unbearable despair that I gave in. I stopped taking medications, and, well, here I am now. There was a day that I looked at myself in the mirror, so lifeless and pointless, and I remember calling out to God, 'Is this what you want from me? Is this my purpose here on this earth?' To my surprise, I heard someone respond, 'Yes.' I looked to my right and my left and saw no one. In the mirror, I looked again. A light surrounded my countenance, like a halo, and it was as if someone had lifted the cloud from my heart."

Her finger twitched upon my arm once, and she gazed at me seriously. "Life is too short," she began, "To be weighed down by worry. There will come a day when I will have perfect little fingers and feet that can walk, dance, and leap. But for now, I am happy because I trust that one day that day will come."

To trust is to give. To give is to lose. When you give something away, you aren't expecting it back. It isn't as if you can rent it out and have it returned to your property with the name signed neatly on the paper. Is that not what consecration is? To consecrate is to make something holy, so why not declare yourself so? Are you not a chosen and sacred vessel? Take a good hard look at yourself in the mirror and truly ask yourself, like Turian, "Is this what you want from me?" The gospel is true because God can not lie. It is impossible for him to do so.

Someday, Turian will fall down at Christ's feet. She will tenderly touch his scarred feet, marred by the sting of the cross. Those dove-colored eyes will cling to his robe as an ocean of gratitude cascades down her face.

I hope I will be with her. There are times when I wonder, I'm so flawed. I am afraid far too often, and yet, I can't help but dip into her faith. She is so compelling not because of her physical strength but because of her commitment to Him.

Journal – Contemplate this: Where are you now in your relationship with Jesus Christ? Are you distant? Close? When I capsize in the daze of my endless thoughts, I reach for a branch. I call it my final push, like that ultimate breath of air I take before I tumble under the surface. As I scream into the indigo depths, I remember I can swim. Barely. Just the dog paddle. Spiritually, when my reserves are depleted, I tell the Lord I will give Him something – my widow's mite. Whether that be leaving a kind note on my neighbor's door or deciding to read the scriptures, I give it to him.

In this journal entry, I invite you to do the same. Maybe you've been driving on fumes for the past couple of miles. Humor me with this experiment. Ask God for His mercy as you give your ultimate effort to sink or swim. Again and again, I have seen Him pull me out of the water and bring me back to the world of the living.

Honesty:

I will say this now: this book may hurt before it heals. Fear is an addiction, a coping mechanism for anxiety that seems safe but really isn't. It's a gaping chasm. It sucks the joy out of relationships and saps the zest out of life. DO NOT STAY HERE. Perfectionism is most often linked to a sense of low self-esteem, even from people who have always been popular, witty, or smart. What I'm asking you to do is to be vulnerable with yourself because the first step in eliminating fear is acknowledging that it exists within you.

Start with the thoughts. What do you think about yourself, really? Behind all of the accomplishments, what do you see in yourself? What is the lie, and what is the truth? It's time to untangle the fishing line and get down to the reality of your situation.

"Truth can not be altered by the opinions of men…if men are really humble, they will realize that they discover, but do not create truth." -Spencer W. Kimball

It's time to discover the truth.

JESUS CHRIST AND YOUR IDENTITY

My truth begins here: I am a toxic perfectionist.

Sometimes, even deeper than the thoughts and feelings that you have, you need to go back to your identity and how you see yourself. I will explain. I clawed my way toward the letter "A." I was smart in high school, so why couldn't I be in college? With tight fists and a racing mind, I studied all day and well into the night. In the first semester, I achieved high A's in my classes and praise from my professors, who applauded me for my dedication to learning. In the second semester, the same story happened: straight As in every class. The third semester began to wear on me. The nursing program loomed over me like a black cloud, strengthening my obsession to reach some unattainable goal. To get into the nursing program, I "needed" to accomplish straight A's (though this was not necessarily true). I felt trapped. Every time I

17

went in to take a test, I honestly could never see myself succeeding. I felt like if I did not study, cram, and give every waking hour to my classes, I would lose my dream. In a way, my dreams have always driven me. I've always been a huge dreamer. My ideas for life are huge! But if I let go of my way of thinking, what if I didn't achieve my dreams? What if I messed up? What if I really wasn't capable of doing anything that I had longed for my entire existence?

There came a day when I was sitting with my fiance watching a movie when this crashing avalanche of doubt filled my mind. Not of him, not of God, but of myself. The feeling had visited before, one that I refused to acknowledge but always seemed to push its way through – that I hated myself. Now, hate is a strong word, and I always tried to deny that pithy expression, but if I wanted to overcome it, I had to confess its existence. This is called self-honesty to overcome recrimination. And when those feelings of self-hate came on the strongest, I flailed, devastatingly determined to love my fiance as much as I knew I had the potential to do. It frustrated me because I shoved it down, seemed to overcome it, and it would suddenly emerge again like a ground squirrel burrowing through my system and popping up exactly when I didn't want it. I never truly desired its presence, that self-loathing, but time and time again, it reared its ugly head.

To put the self-hatred at bay, I began with the only thing I knew. Writing. Something deep within me told me my story needed to be written.

It all started with works of fiction. Long sweeping paragraphs with endless lines of stories about heroes and dragons, princesses, and magic. I was terrified to show the world how I felt. In truth, sometimes I didn't even know how to explain it. Spy stories and great tragedies that's what the people want, right? What could my life matter to the world? I'm pretty ordinary. Brown hair and green eyes. I can't reach the top shelf without standing on my tippy toes. But there was something calling me. Out there. In the great unknown, stretching me, urging me to look beyond the person I saw standing in the mirror. Was it possible that I could attain this?

Luke 1:37, "For with God nothing shall be impossible."

Then I saw it. What did it matter what the world thought of me? Could it be possible that God saw within me what I only viewed in glimpses of my mere mortal life (Jeremiah 1:5, Alma 26:35)? Could it be that HE believed I could do it? An overwhelming, tear-inducing love thronged my chest. Thick and heavy, like one of those thick winter quilts you curl up in when your world is falling apart. I could feel it. It was real, tangible love. It consumed me, and for a moment, the universe seemed to be pointing in my direction, yielding every possible evidence that I, indeed, was God's most exquisite creation.

"Our conviction that God made a mistake is shaped by our inability to see the utterly ingenious purpose that lays behind His design. And we don't see that purpose because our focus is riveted on the effort to correct something that was never wrong."-Craig D. Lounsbrough[4]

Christlike Meditation:[5]

Throughout this book, I want to provide you with ways that you may gain an advantage over your fear. According to the Cleveland Clinic, mediation "involves focusing or clearing your mind using a combination of mental and physical techniques." Over thousands of years, this process of letting everything meld into one introspective moment. My husband was actually the one who introduced me to this while we were dating, and at the time, I thought it was a little strange. One man was talking really slowly while my husband and I breathed deeply in and out and tried not to think about the crazy world around us. However, months later, I knew I needed something more to change.

Thanks to extensive psychological research, we know that attitudes stem from certain behaviors and determine how the information changes into a responding action.[6] There are many different forms of meditation, which will be highlighted and described in this book. You don't have to be Mahatma Gandhi to do it; all you have to do is stop and listen.

J. Donald Walters, a successful guru in the art of mindful thinking, stated, "The more regularly and the more deeply you meditate, the sooner you will find yourself always acting from a center of peace."

Jesus Christ himself spent his time in silence. For forty days and forty nights, he fasted and prayed, delving into that inner strength that he would later need to undergo the Atonement (Luke 4:1-13). After his cousin John the Baptist lost his life at the hands of merciless oppressors, Christ retreated into the wilderness to find his divine center again. We all have the glowing core of divinity within us. It is the light of Christ. But sometimes, in the hustle and bustle of our days, we lose ourselves. That core gets left in a box in the closet to be forgotten. Meditation allows us to find that balance again, that midline between earthly life and the celestial destiny of all.

When I feel overwhelmed, I meditate. When I feel worried, I meditate. I take myself out of the problem, out of my world, and face it with an outsider's perspective. All of a sudden, I'm not so afraid anymore because I can see my Savior at my side. What I am asking you to do now is to let go of the steering wheel for one moment. Remember our analogy at the beginning of the book? For this moment in time, allow Christ to drive. Let him fill you with his matchless power. (Mosiah 4:6) You are limitless with his love.

So, let's begin here and now.

I encourage you to start a five-minute timer here, and as we practice and improve, continue to lengthen your time.

Begin by taking in a deep breath, letting your stomach fill with air. Slowly release it. In and out, steady and calm, like the gently lapping waves of the ocean, drawing in and pushing out. In and out. Steady and calm. Do this until you feel any tightness in your chest dissipates. (The first time should extend no more than 5 minutes). This form of meditation heavily relies upon repeating one phrase over and over. Gravitate towards this thought. If your mind drifts away, quietly call it back to this one phrase. Continue to breathe, in and out, steady and calm. Allow the tightness in your neck, arms, and fingers to slowly disappear. In and out, steady and calm. Perfect. Now, as you continue to breathe, focus on this phrase, "I am enough." If you don't quite believe it yet, that is okay. Repeat it with the intake of your breath, "I am enough."

Marianne Williamson stated, "Our deepest fear is not that we are inadequate. Our deepest fear is that we are powerful beyond measure. It is our light, not our darkness that most frightens us. We ask ourselves, 'Who am I to be brilliant, gorgeous, talented, fabulous?' Actually, who are you not to be? You are a child of God. Your playing small does not serve the world. There is nothing enlightened about shrinking so that other people won't feel insecure around you. We are all meant to shine, as children do. We were born to make manifest the glory of God that is within us. It's not just in some of us; it's in everyone. And as we let our own light shine, we unconsciously give other people permission to do the same. As we are liberated from our own fear, our presence automatically liberates others."[7]

Enough of "enough."

What does the word enough even mean? A year ago, I couldn't have told you. I knew how badly I craved it from my parents, my peers, my God. If I could be enough for them… well, then what? It was some mindless marathon towards a future goal that was constantly outpacing my strides. It tasted sweet on my tongue to say the word FLAWLESS. If you want to see fear at its finest, ask it what it thinks of you. Scoffing, it will give you the once over and say, "Not enough."

I want you to just say that to yourself out loud. "I am good, and that is enough."

We all live with an inner voice in our heads. Too much self-criticism can lead to depression or self-loathing! Self-care seems too similar to self-pity. Why is it so difficult to cut ourselves some slack? How do you take care of your friends? Who is your best friend right now? Are you being a friend to yourself? Why do we not protect us from us?? To be able to defend ourselves from the powers surrounding us (our circumstances), we have to stand on our own side. Our real enemy begins inside of us. If you are hurt by the words of others, is it because you worry they are right? We start creating a different persona in our heads than what we may actually demonstrate on the outside. We hear people breathing and assume they think we are nothing because that is what we feel we are internally.

We begin taunting our enemy, saying that we despise ourselves more than they could ever loathe us.

Sometimes, when help comes, we even principally shove it away. Why would they bother helping someone beyond repair? This process is about rewiring the system.

Teaching your mind to love… You're horrible. You are worthless. You are an idiot. The words in your head are simply a meaningless cacophony of bird calls from other people. They originated with them. And now they are buried in you. There are good ones and bad ones. Absorb the good voices and ditch the bad ones.

Alice

Breathe. Alice told herself. Breathe. But she couldn't. The air constricted in her lungs, and she dipped under the surface again. The walls closed in. The world turned on its side. Alice couldn't do it. No, she absolutely could not. The tears burned hot and bright as my sister slipped into the fresh supply of attacks she stored in her private warehouse. Like a slap to the face, the words, "You aren't good enough," permeated the armor she girded around every exterior.

She worked so hard to reach this point. Every day for nearly a year and a half, studying and cramming to enter the nursing program. Everyone was so proud of her. All she wanted to do was succeed, and she earned her goal. Or had she? The victory echoed a hollow hum now. The nursing program lay before her, a galaxy of unknowns. Everyone expected her to do this. Her whole life, Alice always expected herself to succeed. But what was success at this point? Quitting wasn't an option, but she longed to escape. Six assignments lay in front of her, due before midnight, and it was already 8 o'clock. Like the base drop in a rock concert, Alice's mind vibrated with thoughts careening into one another and imploding.

In the solitude of her apartment, she cried out, "I hate this."

There was no one there to hear.

Surrounded by a table of other frayed-haired nursing students, their eyes heavy from the level of effort they exerted daily to maintain their spot in the nursing program, Alice resisted her desire to melt into the floor. What was she doing here? Day in and day out, fighting for something so intensely difficult? A tutor swept into the room, her bright eyes a blaze with something the bone-tired students desperately needed: hope. Pounding his fist on the table, a tutor nearly shouted, "Remember how much you wanted this. Why are you here?"

A flash of a memory entered Alice's mind. A teary-eyed woman could only shed tears of joy as two student nurses bathed and adjusted her to save her weak body from bed sores. She saw little boys and girls who could no longer walk as the plague of cancer multiplied and devoured their extremities. The woman in labor. The blind man. The malnourished nations. She saw them all, and in the midst of it, she saw herself. It should have overwhelmed her, but a wave of peace washed over her soul before it seemed to be the perfect storm. Ten 100-point assignments were due at the end of every day. But in the eye of the storm was her reason to continue. She had every reason to succeed. And if she didn't, it would be ok.

WHAT WOULD CHRIST SAY TO ME IF HE KNEW ME?

With permission, I'm sharing the account of one of my good friends while she attended a girls' camp in the summer. I always knew when I arrived at our single ward activity on Monday night that, I would be greeted with a sly grin from Libby. Without fail, the girl from Virginia lightened my evening, no matter how tired and overwhelmed I felt even seconds before.

Libby recounts that as all of the fun activities of the day winded to a close, the girls lined up in rows and awaited the instructions of their leaders. The game was simple. Dedicated young women leaders called out for the girls to each close their eyes and think about the part of their body assigned. For example, if the head was called, each girl pondered about how she personally regarded her face, her hair, and her nose. Continuing down the body, Libby knew that she didn't have the perfect figure, nor did she necessarily love other portions of herself as well. She peeked open an eyelid and looked around. Was everyone else feeling as inadequate as she was? After completing the grueling self-evaluation, the young women president asked the young women to open their eyes.

Beckoning each girl close, she gently described how the Savior felt about his brothers and sisters. In our heads, he sees a brain full of potential, thoughts that will spark new generations of innovation. He sees our eyes, so tender and anxious to fulfill our destinies. Our hearts, which pump vital, life-saving oxygen even to the extremities of our fingertips and pinky toes, desire to reach out to others. In mercy, the Savior sees our hands and, in them, his own (Jeremiah 18:6).

Libby stared down at her own hands, dejection crushing her with every word. How desperately she longed to believe the endless praise sung in her name. Could it really be true that the most perfect being in the universe regarded her as such? The young teenager didn't know if she could believe it.

Then, in an instant, her mind opened to something much bigger than herself. She heard a voice calling her by name. Libby couldn't lift her gaze from her hands. Something inside of her snarled at their imperfection, how the folds of skin didn't sit quite right, the nails short and chewed. A tear brushed her cheek. The voice called her name again; then two perfect hands settled on top of hers. Two perfect scars, ten perfect fingers, and one perfect Savior. Libby looked up to see him.

Jesus Christ smiled. He wiped away the single tear trickling down his sister's face and said, "You are enough for me. Remember your worth, Libby."

ROOTS

If you hate yourself, you will melt under the heat of other people's words

I never thought I would assimilate so much to cheese. Scrape, scrape, scrape against the cheese grater. When it's not being shredded, it's being sliced. We crumble it, mix it, and then buy a new block to start all over again. I tried not to look like a weirdo as I stared at someone grating a block of cheese, imagining myself putting myself through the same mangling process. It's not that I want to. Or mean to. Or like to. I just do. Sometimes I don't like myself, but it's okay. But it didn't used to be.

I covered up my stunted self-esteem for years. I buried it, joking about my weight, about what a "failure" I was, and how my eyebrows were too thick. I dug the hole, and then I climbed right in and kept digging. It's funny, but if you've ever dug your own crater before, you find a variety of things. Moles and earthworms, tiny underground streams, but above all of that, roots. I read once that roots bind the tree to the soil, providing it with water from the subterranean reserves. Fairfax County says that "eighty percent of all roots occur in the top 12-36 inches of soil."[8] Some trees have the potential to develop more extensive roots if they are put into

26

the right dirt. These are taproots, which save the tree from windy days and periods of drought.

I've been told before that I have an overactive imagination. I see things and assimilate to them. I used to hide it because I was embarrassed that I felt so similar to random objects in my life. But this analogy has stuck with me. The deeper I dug my hole to conceal my low self-esteem, the more I came back to my roots. Hitting a root with your shovel basically signals the end of your excavation, at least until you can find a saw or something other than your dull spade to get through it. Ideally, roots are supposed to support you if they grow in the correct soil.

I wish my soil had been perfectly fertilized to make my roots dive deep, but in a lot of ways, my roots are growing in very shallow sand.

The more I looked back on how I was raised, the experiences I went through, and the expectations I held for myself, the more I wished they would disappear. I was embarrassed by how anxious and lonely I had become. More than anything, I just wanted to be normal. But my tree was not growing healthily the way it was, and it took some digging to find that out. If I continued to uncover and expose my roots, they would die for lack of water. Because I didn't understand that I was needed and wanted, all I wanted to do was keep hiding in the cool earth with my roots. But I was killing myself. I was destroying what had taken my entire life to grow.

It was time to accept what was keeping me alive. My history.

So, I drew this diagram. It is a reflection of everything I have shared with you within this chapter: my feelings, blended together with my life story, all written into a tree. I found myself, what I actually thought of myself, the things I said when I lay awake at night crying to the ceiling. They are ugly thoughts, repressed slandering written and taken to the press in my personal New York Times. Things I exerted every endeavor to hide.

But in order for me to fertilize my roots, I had to change my mindset. My tree twisted sideways as the cyclones of life beat down on it. I had to rebuild. I had to regrow. So I did. And then I decided I wanted you to do the same.

Dieter F. Uchdorf said, "...being able to see ourselves clearly is essential to our spiritual growth and well-being. If our weaknesses and shortcomings remain obscured in the shadows, then the redeeming power of the Savior cannot heal them and make them strengths. Ironically, our blindness toward our human weaknesses will also make us blind to the divine potential that our Father yearns to nurture within each of us." [9]

I asked God to help me cure my tree. The roots were rotting away, and the leaves were beginning to yellow. I thought by camouflaging myself under the ground, I would be sheltered. But it was cold, damp, and lonely down there. The only way to save my future was to come to grips with who I was.

Christian Lewis said, "The Christian does not think God will love us because we are good, but that God will make us good because He loves us."[10]

So, once again, I wrote. And rewrote. Then, I rewrote again. Jesus Christ is the author and finisher of our faith (Hebrews 12:2, Moroni 6:4).

How you feel is not who you are.

What you do is not who you are.

How I sometimes feel:

Worthless

Stupid

Workaholic

Obsessed about things I shouldn't be

A chronic crier

Like I missed the mark

Not pretty

Not athletic

Not smart

Not good enough for Nathan

Not good enough for God

What I sometimes do:

FFA

Basketball

4H

Track and Field

Cross Country

Writing

Drawing

Serving others

Attending church

Lifting

Adventuring

Who I am:

Daughter of Seth and Erin Larson

21 years old (pretty young, lot's to learn)

Love to sing, and it's ok if I don't have a voice like Taylor Swift

I'm an artist, not a perfect one, but one who loves to share

My smile, when real, infuses my own soul with joy

I love serving others

I get frustrated sometimes because I want to help so many other people, but I realize now that it is ok to let myself rest sometimes.

I love public speaking and expressing my beliefs

I love meeting new people and learning their interests

I am a talented athlete who loves to be active

I am a good student who loves to learn

Journal: Start with your roots. Pictured below. Write within the roots how you feel and who you are.

It is time to rewrite your story.

Journal: Begin writing things you like about yourself. If you can think of nothing, ask someone else to write some things for you. Look at those words. Stare them down and ask yourself if you are worthy of being loved. Then, even if you don't believe it, force yourself to say yes. Yes, I am wonderful, talented, and needed. I belong here. My weaknesses do not define me. My anxiety, depression, OCD, or any other problem is NOT who I am. Look at yourself in the mirror. Admire the wrinkles, lines, and curves of your face, how you are distinctly individual from every other person on the planet. God made you to be you.

Your
Roots

Sources

1) Kwong, Emily. "Understanding Unconscious Bias : Short Wave." *NPR.org*, 15 July 2020, www.npr.org/2020/07/14/891140598/understanding-unconscious-bias.

2) Kelly, Owen. "Ignoring Obsessions Actually Makes OCD Worse." *Verywell Mind*, June 2021, www.verywellmind.com/thought-suppression-and-ocd-2510480.

3) Sawchuk, Craig. "Depression (Major Depressive Disorder)." *Mayo Clinic*, Mayo Foundation for Medical Education and Research, 14 Oct. 2022, www.mayoclinic.org/diseases-conditions/depression/symptoms-causes/syc-20356007.

4) *A quote by Craig D. Lounsbrough*. (2024). Goodreads.com. https://www.goodreads.com/quotes/11328200-our-conviction-that-god-made-a-mistake-is-shaped-by

5) Cleveland Clinic. (2022, May 22). *Meditation*. Cleveland Clinic; Cleveland Clinic. https://my.clevelandclinic.org/health/articles/17906-meditation

6) MacKinnon, D. P., Fairchild, A. J., & Fritz, M. S. (2007). Mediation Analysis. *Annual Review of Psychology*, *58*(1), 593–614.

7) Williamson, M. (2016). *A Return to Love*. HarperOne.

8) Fairfax County. (n.d.). *Understanding Tree Roots | Northern Virginia Soil and Water Conservation District*. Www.fairfaxcounty.gov. https://www.fairfaxcounty.gov/soil-water-conservation/understanding-tree-roots

9) Uchtdorf, D. F. (2014, October). *"Lord, Is It I?"* Www.churchofjesuschrist.org. https://www.churchofjesuschrist.org/study/general-conference/2014/10/lord-is-it-i?lang=eng

10) Lewis, C. S. (2009). *Mere Christianity*. HarperCollins UK.

CHAPTER 2: REST

When my dad read chapter one of this book, he told me I needed to bring more levity into the story. And it's true. It's not realistic to say that I am always drowning in my despair or so hopeless that I don't know how I'll continue.

John 16:22 says, "And ye now therefore have sorrow: but I will see you again, and your heart shall rejoice, and your joy no man taketh from you."

I've seen so many miracles in my life. I have felt true joy, and so have you (Isaiah 29:19, 2 Nephi 2:25). Mists of darkness may cover it up at times (1 Nephi 8:24), but the sun is waiting to shine in your life. Sometimes, it is more difficult to ingest the jubilation when I am unsure of who I am trying to be. We learned in Chapter 1 about the importance of returning to our roots. With that comes acknowledging all parts of our human nature: good and bad, selfish and selfless, brave and terrified (Philippians 4:8). That is step two to overcoming fear, so I am making a declaration right here, right now.

I fart sometimes.

I know, horrible, right? For some reason, among females, it is completely obscene to release gas, and if the deed is done in public, the doer is publicly humiliated by capital punishment. That may be a bit dramatic, but in junior high, it was not.

If I ever created any flatulence near my peers, I never, ever admitted it. EVER. It was so disgusting and mortifying that I even sometimes accused someone next to me of being the *farter* to escape my crimes (Doctrine and Covenants 3:7).

So, I'm a flawed person (and a stinky one). Does that gross you out? Are you uncomfortable? Me too!

Just as I continually decline to admit that I am a stinky *farter*, I often refuse to recognize the parts of myself that I don't like.

It reminds me of a child I once observed on a hot Indian summer day, her eyes dancing with the grandeur of a local parade.

I noticed the child after the procession ended. She dove her chubby palm into her Walmart grocery sack and pulled out a handful of sweets. The young girl held the treasures close to her eyes, so close that I wondered if she could see anything. Then, she methodically tossed away what she had.

"Nope." She pronounced in disgust, tossing a double bubblegum.

Next went the lemon head. While her parents chatted amiably with their neighbors, the little girl chucked her candy back into the road to be crushed by passing cars.

Sixlets. Crunch. Into the street.

Swedish fish. Crunch.

On went the list of discarded confectionery to be executed by the oncoming cars. I couldn't help but giggle because *I* would have liked to have some of that sugar she tossed so flippantly away. Eventually, the child's mother noticed what was happening and grabbed the sticky arm of her picky kid.

Sometimes, I try to pick the parts of myself that I like the best. The sweet ones, the ones that everyone else likes too. Many times, I don't even *want to sample* the other bars in my bag because I'm scared I won't like them or maybe others won't like them. So, as the Fourth of July kindergartener, I throw those parts far, far away, hoping they will be run over by a car and disappear. The fact that

I can release an odor more potent than mustard gas from my behind is not something I'm necessarily proud of. So I throw it away, never to be seen again. Or so I think.

But the story didn't end there. When the mania of people returning to their homes ceased, the child's mother towed her girl onto the cracked pavement. This brave soul helped her child clean up every single piece she discarded, which she then put back into her bag.

I laughed. The pieces came back a little dirty and a little smashed, but back inside the Walmart sack.

Sometimes I don't even recognize that I am feeling stressed, sad, anxious, angry, or lonely because it doesn't fit who I want to be. I toss away the bad and keep the good, but the bad has a way of resurfacing. And you know what? It's ok that it does.

Psalm 46:10 says, "Be still, and know that I am God: I will be exalted among the heathen, I will be exalted in the earth."

The problem was that I needed to slow my cadence to feel better. I was trying to sprint a marathon despite my dehydration and lack of training. I like to go fast. I'm a solver and a builder. I try to help others all that I can, but in constantly moving like a madwoman, I get lost in doing instead of living.

Aubrey Johnson, a writer about mental health, stated, "As young adults, I think the majority of us struggle with loving ourselves and finding joy within ourselves. It starts off with not thinking very positively about our bodies, our personalities, or our abilities. Once we have figured out exactly what it is we don't like (which, unfortunately, is far too easy), we try to change those things. But maybe that change doesn't happen fast enough or in the way we were hoping. Or we start comparing ourselves to others on social media, and then we feel miserable all over again. Sadly, a lot of us will brood in self-pity and all of our perceived "flaws" instead of trying to find joy within ourselves." [1]

Stillness can lead to joy because we can process what we feel (Ecclesiastes 3:1-8). Who cares if you are jealous of your older brother because he always did everything right? Why not feel that resentment you have built up towards the person who first abused you? How can you not shout with exhilaration as you fly down a whirlwind of a roller coaster ride? Yes, the Savior asked us to be perfect, but to be perfect in Hebrew means to be whole (Matthew 5:48, 3 Nephi 12:48). That means that the Only Begotten Son of God will clasp your hand in his and pull you out onto that cracked pavement. Like the little girl, you may exclaim to him that you don't want your rejected candy. That's why you tossed it away in the first place! Then, you will truly feel like a small child with a big brother.

Jesus Christ will say to you, "I want you to be with me. All of you. Every single part. Because I suffered for every fragment of your being. You are mine."

Then he will mercifully place your renounced parts of who you are. Because that is what he does. He reclaims what was lost (Luke 15:11-24).

Losing and Finding

Ava stepped onto the edge of the mountainside, her breath coming out in white puffs. She scoured the snowy hillside, hoping to catch a glimpse of a lost cow. Ava was about to continue down the trail to keep her body warm. Shivering, she pulled the collar of her jacket tighter against her neck. They needed to locate the calf before dark. The November sky slipped its wintry chill into her sleeves, and Ava stared at the ponderosa pines that jutted up into the sky like nature's skyscrapers. Something told Ava to stay.

From her perch above the expansive valley, she could see everything. Her eyes burned from the frigid wind, so she closed them and absorbed the stillness. God's stillness.

A scripture came to her mind: Psalm 46, "Be still and know that I am God."

Ava inhaled the sky, rippling with shades of amber and scarlet. Motionless, she simply was. Her chest rose up and down. The calf was still lost from its mother. Ava did not know where it was, nor did anyone else who populated this sparse landscape. Lost.

Ava knew what it was to be lost (Matthew 15:24). Biting her lip, her emotion smothered the breath from her throat. For too long, the feeling of aimlessness pitted her with pockmarks of isolation.

Where would she go when she was lost? There were times Ava wished to remain here, like the bear, antelope, and wolves roaming the countryside (John 8:32). Sometimes, others didn't understand her. Many times. Too often, her heart pulsed, ripping a cavern in her chest. Sleep evaded her with a defiant stance, allowing her memories to rack her mind with a battery of her mistakes and her future responsibilities.

As Ava hesitated in this sacred spot, her soul found rest (Jacob 1:7). Safety. Maybe even love. It was difficult for her to feel it sometimes. Hard to explain and even harder to comprehend. Of course, she was happy. Ava had every reason to be. But then, too often, the alarm returned. She feared too often. Yet, too often, she didn't know how to escape.

Glimpsing the area around her and finding no one, Ava brushed away the silt and knelt to offer a prayer. It was simple and awkward, and she knew that others could speak more eloquently than she. But Ava thanked God regardless for providing her a place of stillness.

Question: Where do you find your stillness? How can you put yourself in a place to hear God more?

Karen Conlon, the founder of Cohesive NYC Therapy, said, "Rest looks and feels different for different people, and I don't think there's necessarily one particular explanation for what rest can look like. Our minds and our bodies are connected, not just through physiology but also through ways of communicating. I think that it is so important for people to wrap their heads around and try to accept that you can't take care of one without taking care of the other. They're always in communication, informing each other what condition one is in." [2]

Running from What

It pains me sometimes to slow down, to discover that stillness. I almost feel as though I am doing something wrong.

I was always running in my dreams. Same dream, different bad guys, every night for five years. I used to joke that I had those dreams because of my constant training for track and cross country, but deep down, I knew I was not just running; I was fleeing (Jonah 1:1-4). It took me a long time to figure out what it was from.

My throat aches from tamping down the vomit climbing my throat. They're coming for me. I know it. I can't escape them. Who are they? It varies from night to night. Sometimes, it's a gang of mercenaries; other times, the police accusing me of a crime I didn't commit. I creep under an old cardboard box as their shouts grow nearer. Curling my knees up to my chest, I question if I will die in the place, small and helpless. Then, I make a decision. With all of my might, I leap from hiding and sprint, commanding my legs to pound harder, faster (1 Corinthians 9:24). And I wake up running.

One night, I had this dream again. It began like the regular neighborhood nightmare, but this time it was different. I was swimming in a sea of human bodies pressed tightly against each other. Some were screeching, pushing to run in one direction while others reached their hands out in the other. I moved with the stronger current. Claustrophobia burrowed into my skin, and I moved more quickly to escape the swirling crowd (Doctrine and Covenants 10:4-5).

The thought came to my mind, "Where am I running to? Who am I running from?"

I paused in the center of Times Square, being jostled and bumped but unmoving. Then I turned around. He was there. Jesus Christ. Standing at the end of the long cobbled street. So many were running away from him, like me, not even bothering to glance back. He lifted his scarred hand towards me and said, "Come" (John 1:46).

I could only stare in wonder. A few people cried out to him, "Lord, Lord!" The Savior began to move towards me. Most didn't even glance in his direction, hurrying on, but those who were waiting for him created a path as the lamb of God silently approached me (Proverbs 4:12). I fell at his feet and sobbed. For so long, I had been making a break for it. I ran and ran. Were my feet bleeding? Yes! Did I long to stop? Of course! Most times, I didn't even completely know where my ending place would be. I simply woke to a blaring alarm and sweat beading down my spine.

How silly! How futile the race had been! If I had simply looked back in that repetitive dream, I know I would have seen him there.

The thought had never occurred to me before.

We are all attempting to escape something. It could be a bad breakup. Maybe a chain of bad decisions or an abusive childhood.

When we are wrapped in all-encompassing fear, it is difficult to understand the phrase "direction over speed."

You may say to me now, "Emree, don't tell me how to run away! I want to hightail it out of here faster than a greased pig with its tail on fire!" (I would be mildly entertained if you *did* say that to me.)

I was running from me: from my past, present, and future. But I wasn't running to anybody! I was circling uselessly, and Satan loved it!

Running has its place if we know where we are running to. Let it be Christ. He's holding out his arms for you. Isn't it remarkable that when he perished on the cross, his arms were stretched out (Isaiah 5:25, Jacob 6:4)? Even when he was at the peak of his suffering, he offered his love for us. If you simply pause, even for the tiniest of moments, you will see that he is the direction to which you must turn. Running does you no good without a destination. You will become one of the world's many wanderers. Purposeless. Meaningless. Lifeless.

Meditation Moment:

Let's move on to a new form of meditation. I call it being divinely present. Following the same pattern as the last meditation moment, let your breaths fall in slow, even waves (1 Samuel 1:15). Thoughts may come and go as they please in your mind, like a giant highway of positive energy. You don't live in the past. You don't live in the future. You live in the present. Try to slow the thoughts to an even pace. These ideas may pass in and out of your mind, but they do not drive you. You do. In and out, ever so slowly, breathe. Allow yourself to inhale and exhale, even for a few seconds, deeply and fully (Mosiah 7:33). If your lungs constrict, I encourage you to repeat a comforting phrase in your mind such as,

"God will not abandon me" or "God is on my side" or "I am not afraid." (I will leave that part up to your discretion).

Focus on your breathing. If you feel the worry and doubt creeping in, let it come. Allow those thoughts to simply be. You are in control of your life. Breathe in and out, in and out. Do this over and over again. Allow the world you live in to bathe your consciousness. You do not have anywhere to be right now. Let the past and future fade for a moment. When you are finished here, imagine the sensations of the following… (feel free to think of your own as well)

Smell the freshly cut green grass. Breathe in and out, in and out.

Touch the bricks of an old stone building. Breathe in and out, in and out.

Taste the spicy crispness of the fall air. In and out, in and out.

Listen to the melody of kids playing, cars beeping, or even the sound of silence. In and out, in and out.

Watch a bird bring a wriggling worm back to its nest. In and out, in and out.

There is power in stillness.

"Peace, peace, be still."

God made this perfect symphony of hallowed grace for you to understand his majesty. When we race with our lives flying at one hundred miles per hour, the music gets lost in the madness.

Stop and ask yourself here: what direction are my thoughts taking me? Do I know? Who am I running to?

THE DAY I WENT TO COUNSELING

My direction wasn't heading towards Jesus. I was hurtling towards the edge of a cliff, a thousand-foot drop awaiting me (Moses 7:57). I didn't want to fall, so I turned to the only thing I hadn't tried: therapy. The word made me shudder. All my life, I have heard that only the most shattered individuals have entered that office.

On the day of my first appointment, sweat poured out of my pits like Niagara Falls. I pasted my spine to the back of my hard chair, consciously commanding my leg not to bounce. I felt like everyone was watching me. Somehow, I needed to protect myself from judgment. Discreetly, I smelled my armpit. Yikes, that was some serious BO. I bit my lip and tried to look sane. It was a nice office, and I grappled to calm myself down. What was my problem? It was just therapy! I wasn't going to donate my kidney or get a blood transfusion!

My stomach knotted itself into a twisty straw (Genesis 3:9-11). Four children poked each other and giggled, playing with various toys the therapists left for them. Their parents shouted in the other room. The oldest boy had tear stains on his cheeks.

What was I doing here? I had never told anyone except for my husband the depth of my emotions! I liked being a happy-go-lucky little jelly bean! Nobody knew anything different about me. The problem was that I wasn't sure how to separate my true identity from the smiley face mask.

Then, the dreaded moment. The therapist emerged and summoned me. I felt like a zoo animal, but I acted like I was at ease. Totally cool. My breathing was similar to that of a congested gorilla. My smell wasn't much better.

I've always had a hard time telling others I'm treading water, that my head is barely afloat. But as I conversed with my therapist,

I nearly balked at how calm she was. Words spewed out of my mouth, creating stories and memories of a person. Me. She just listened. Then, after a long moment, she told me what a good job I was doing.

People told me that before, but I fought it. Like a lizard pouncing on an unsuspecting bug, I chomped down the praise to be digested and didn't think about it anymore. I couldn't. I didn't have time to dwell on how good I was doing because I had so much more to improve.

Her words pierced me to the core. Was I doing enough? Was I improving as much as she said I was? I reflected for several minutes before I spoke again. For years, I abandoned a part of myself in the shadows. Few people knew the true me because I didn't want them to. In that moment, however, one more person did. She was my second safety buddy.

I had been told before that going to therapy meant you were severed beyond repair, that your life was in such shambles because you never figured out how to fix it yourself. That was the pride in me. To me, therapy meant failure to thrive.

How wrong I was! I expected to feel uncomfortable sharing my feelings and my "craziness" with other people. But as I blew my nose into another crumpled Kleenex, I was surprised at the freedom I felt (John 8:32). A load fell from my shoulders, one that I bore for too long.

As I pondered on the experience, I wondered how long I had been trying to disguise myself from God, to bury my ugliness under a rock. It wouldn't work, of course, but I attempted it nonetheless. I worried that if I never overcame my anxiety or my perfectionism, God may never be proud of me. It came from a misunderstanding of who my Father in Heaven truly was.

My Dad

My husband says we think of our Heavenly Father like our earthly Father. For a long time, I believed God would never be proud of me, no matter what I did. Unfortunately, this thought stemmed from what I thought about my Dad.

Letter from my Dad (2023)

"Hey Emree, I am happy to hear how many little miracles that you see in your work. God has been blessing you with those little miracles from as far back as I can remember in your life. Learning to recognize and be humble and grateful for them is a spiritual gift you have. You will be able to find brightness in your life even when everything around you seems dark and gloomy. Keep listening to those promptings and learn to trust God's power. You are learning that he is powerful enough to do all things through you. The secret door to that powerful place is knowing his will. Hearing and acting on inspiration from the Holy Spirit is the key to unlocking it. Helping others to recognize the way God is now or may still prevail in their lives is a great service to them from you. Pray for clarity. When He speaks to you, do not be afraid to speak His thoughts and recognize Him by sharing humble testimony. You are a beautiful, powerful young woman. I love you. DAD."

I grew up always trying to please my dad. He's a man of few words, but I craved his approval and admiration. As the oldest child, I strove to be a good example. Every "good job" was a ray of sunshine for my day. My love language is words of affirmation, while my dad's is quality time. Sometimes, he would take me with him on his hunting trips and tell me stories of his barefoot youth. I loved him so deeply.

As is our tendency as human beings, my thinking patterns drifted to the extreme. In high school, I directed my efforts toward receiving praise and encouragement from others, especially my dad. When my dad corrected me or gave me advice, I splintered. It wasn't his intention to hurt my feelings, but when you're already so hard on yourself, every reproof feels like a bullet through a cardboard box. Over time, seeking to make my dad proud distorted into earning his love. I believed my dad could only be proud of me if I triumphed, and proof of that was his verbal approval. I forgot who my daddy was, and I forgot who I was: his beloved daughter.

This happens too often with mental health. We suppose we are broken beyond repair (Doctrine and Covenants 64:10). We believe God doesn't want or need us now that we have fallen so far. We try to fake it like everything is ok on the outside, but the truth is, we're beginning to wonder if God even cares. Maybe this is a punishment from God for some sin we committed, and now we are paying the price.

All of these notions are valid, but they are false (Psalm 34:8-9). Fear has a way of twisting a little girl's adoration for her father into a desperate lifetime of chasing his love.

Speaking to my dad on the phone, I explained to him how long I languished in my inadequacy. Shame rippled through my trembling hands as I unraveled why I lived this way for so long. All I could get out was, "Daddy, I love you." My internal programming imploded, and I broke down with relief when my father expressed how deeply he adored me. My heart rewinded like a cassette. I remembered carrying my Daddy's boots to him in the morning and seeing him on the track bleachers, cheering me on. Hugging me, Daddy whispered it would be okay when I found out I would have yet another knee surgery. Countless memories I had forgotten, buried under an expectation I had invented. Now I know I don't have to merit anything. My father's love is free (2 Nephi 2:4).

"The perfect, divine expression of fatherhood is our Heavenly Father. His character and attributes include abundant goodness and perfect love. His work and his glory are the development, happiness, and eternal life of His children. Fathers in this fallen world can claim nothing comparable to the Majesty on High, but at their best, they are striving to emulate Him, and they indeed labor in his work. They are honored with a remarkable and sobering trust." -D. Todd Christofferson

Understanding Your Heavenly Father

Hebrews 12:9 says, "Furthermore we have had fathers of our flesh which corrected us, and we gave them reverence: shall we not much rather be in subjection unto the Father of spirits, and live?"

Just as I misunderstood my father and how deeply he cared for me, there are many of you who may wonder the following questions. Where is God (Mosiah 4:9)? Do I matter to him (Psalm 81:10)?

Occasionally, I received God's reassurance that he was proud of me: a warm, encompassing brightness that took away my sorrow, but then that hollow feeling returned. Like my earthly father, I constantly sought reassurance of God's pride for me. Was I doing enough? Would I make it?

J. Dern Cornish stated it beautifully, "Let me be direct and clear. The answers to the questions, 'Am I good enough?' and, 'Will I make it?' are, 'Yes! You are going to be good enough," and, 'Yes, you are going to make it as long as you keep repenting and do not rationalize or rebel.' The God of Heaven is not a heartless referee looking for any excuse to throw us out of the game. He is our perfectly loving Father, who yearns more than anything else to have all of His children come back home and live with Him as families forever. He truly gave His Only Begotten Son that we might not perish but have everlasting life! Please believe, and please take hope and comfort from this eternal truth. Our Heavenly Father intends for us to make it! That is His work and His glory."

Your Heavenly Father is more loving and kind than you can ever imagine (John 17:3). His very reason for existence is to bring you back to him (John 3:16-17). He needs you. I don't think I ever truly understood the depth of how much my Father in heaven loved me until I read this account from Elder Jeffrey R Holland of the Quorum of the Twelve Apostles [3]:

"One Saturday just after his seventh birthday, Brother Barrus's parents promised the family a night at the movies if the chores were done on time. But when young Clyn arrived at the pasture, the cows he sought had crossed the river, even though it was running at a high flood stage. Knowing his rare night at the movies was in jeopardy, he decided to go after the cows himself, even though he had been warned many times never to do so.

As the seven-year-old urged his old horse, Banner, down into the cold, swift stream, the horse's head barely cleared the water. An adult sitting on the horse would have been safe, but at Brother Barrus's tender age, the current completely covered him except when the horse lunged forward several times, bringing Clyn's head above water just enough to gasp for air.

Here, I turn to Brother Barrus's own words:

"When Banner finally climbed the other bank, I realized that my life had been in grave danger and that I had done a terrible thing—I had knowingly disobeyed my father. I felt I could redeem myself only by bringing the cows home safely. Maybe then my father would forgive me. But it was already dusk, and I didn't know for sure where I was. Despair overwhelmed me. I was wet and cold, lost and afraid.

"I climbed down from old Banner, fell to the ground by his feet, and began to cry. Between thick sobs, I tried to offer a prayer, repeating over and over to my Father in Heaven, 'I'm sorry. Forgive me! I'm sorry. Forgive me!'

"I prayed for a long time. When I finally looked up, I saw through my tears a figure dressed in white walking toward me. In the dark, I felt certain it must be an angel sent in answer to my prayers. I did not move or make a sound as the figure approached; I was so overwhelmed by what I saw. Would the Lord really send an angel to me, who had been so disobedient?

"Then a familiar voice said, 'Son, I've been looking for you.' In the darkness, I recognized the voice of my father and ran to his outstretched arms. He held me tightly, then said gently, 'I was worried. I'm glad I found you.'

"I tried to tell him how sorry I was, but only disjointed words came out of my trembling lips—'Thank you … darkness … afraid … river … alone.' Later that night, I learned that when I had not returned from the pasture, my father had come looking for me. When neither I nor the cows were to be found, he knew I had crossed the river and was in danger. Because it was dark and time was of the essence, he removed his clothes down to his long white thermal underwear, tied his shoes around his neck, and swam a treacherous river to rescue a wayward son."

I know that my dad would have done the same thing. Stripping himself of his clothing, he too would have dove into the churning waters in search of me. I know now how much my earthly father loves me now because I asked him. I did the same with God. They love me. And my Father in Heaven loves you, too.

Our God is a being of infinite tenderness. He is not disappointed in your shortcomings. Trust that He is aware of you and that He will answer your prayers if you simply ask.

Try it! Ask God what he thinks of you.

WHO AM I BECOMING?

For so many years, I made it my mission to make Heavenly Father proud. With a white notepad in hand, I scribble down the words "To Do" over a lengthy list. I consider myself an organized person on paper, but in my head, I'm all over the place. I write everything down, then draw a neat little checkbox next to it. Devastation plagued me when I stared down those unmarked boxes (Mosiah 16:4). Then again, it didn't feel much better to check them all off. Even when I completed the list, I was exhausted.

One day in therapy, my counselor grabbed a red expo marker and wrote the familiar words "To Do." My heart pounded at those four letters on the board. My competitive spirit immediately demanded that I complete whatever she wrote, no matter how difficult it may be.

To my surprise, she wrote nothing underneath the words. Shifting to her right, my therapist scrawled the words "To Be." I stared, perplexed. In her even tone, my coach explained to me that "to be" must come before "to do" (Alma 7:7).

The idea fascinated me. All my life, I made lists of things to tackle for the day, the week, and the year. I was pretty good at accomplishing them, but I always ended up with this bare chasm in my chest. Never before had I considered that if I wanted to feel satisfied with what I did, I needed to understand who I wanted to be (John 3:3).

Proverbs 29:18 says, "Where there is no vision, the people perish: but he that keepeth the law, happy is he."

I thought of masks and disguises. On my "To Be" list, I added the word *authentic.* My mind returned to mindless chatter with a plastic smile. *Happy*. Monarch butterflies and mountain bluebells swirled in my memory. Inhaling the colors and smells, I penned the noun *balanced* (Moroni 7:48).

My to-do list ceased to be a meaningless pile of actions. My dreams took shape again. I wrote things on my list that I actually wished to do, like reading a book or cuddling with my husband on the couch. I was more compassionate, more confident, and less stressed. Maybe because I finally had figured out something about stopping to smell the roses. I did like myself! I knew who I wanted to be, and my goals reflected that every single day!

Activity: Write two separate columns. One should be labeled "To Be" and the other "To Do." The "To Be" part will be tricky. Consider your life now. What do you notice? Who do you want to become? You could write attributes like: unselfish, calm, or loving. Then, begin shaping your to-do list to fit the person you wish to become.

TO BE	TO DO

CLEANING THE HOUSE

As mentioned before, the "To Be" list can be a bit daunting. It's uncomfortable and strenuous to rebuild such complex mental architecture, and it often leads to cognitive strain.

I've got news for you. We've all got stress. But there are varying levels that may define how we live or go about our lives. I didn't believe in mental health. I believed in mental strength: the go-getter attitude and the overcomer pride (Proverbs 16:18, 1 Peter 5:5). I believed in athletes standing on podiums, artists presenting their pieces, and rock climbers touching the peak of a 300 ft wall. Those were my idols, but did I truly see them? No. I noted their accomplishments. My entire life was built upon them: the superficial stuff resting gently on the surface when deep down, many of them were suffocating too.

I had to keep pushing. Climbing. Overcoming (Luke 10:48-42). Until I was overcome. This happened quite a bit in my life: the mental breakdowns and the crisis, all attached to my quest for greatness. I thought to myself, "They did it, those great ones. I can be like them. I can push a little harder."

A word of caution on the matter: stress is not best (Psalm 29:11). Are you carrying too much right now? Your mind is like the attic, where you hide all of your antics and family photos, allowing them to be covered in dust. Are you focusing on too many aspects of your house when the attic is unattended? There could be a family of raccoons living there, for all you know. You don't want a water pipe to burst and your ceiling to collapse. It shouldn't take a mental breakdown for you to realize it's time to fix the distress that's cooking up there. If you have time to clean your kitchen, you have time to clean your attic.

Elder Michael A Dunn said, "Instead of trying to perfect everything, what if we tackled just one thing?... Could aggregating small but steady marginal gains in our lives finally be the way to victory over even the most pesky of our shortcomings? Can this bite-sized approach to tackling our blemishes really work? Well, acclaimed author James Clean says this strategy puts the math squarely in our favor. He maintains that "habits are the 'compound interest of self-improvement,' if you can get just one percent better at something each day, by the end of the year... you will be 37 times better." [5]

I know a thing or two about haphazard cleaning. When my husband and I were first married, we slumped into our bed at 3 AM after our magical honeymoon to Hawaii. It was a dazzling experience, but we were happy to be anywhere that didn't hand us peanuts and remind us to fasten our seatbelts. When I woke to our house the next morning I couldn't help but feel claustrophobic. Boxes towered menacingly over us, threatening to fall and crush us with one misstep (Alma 5:19). But it was time for church, so we threw on our Sunday best and stumbled out the door for the two-hour meeting.

School started the next day. I grew accustomed to the clutter but was determined to eventually get rid of it. I greatly respect my mother for raising six rambunctious kids, keeping us fed, watered, and bathed, all while attempting to maintain a tidy house. I had a different kind of homework, and I was up to my ears in it. It seemed that I only had time to barely scrub the kitchen counter and throw the shoes back in the closet before I crawled back into bed. Now, this is a problem I've always possessed. I'm what they call a "spastic cleaner," meaning I buckle down and tidy one corner of the house when something else calls my attention, so I abandon my first task and move on to the next one. I have this vision that, somehow, I'm going to have the time and stamina to achieve my goal. Rarely does it happen. My cluttered house continued to look like a landfill for nearly a month and a half, all because I couldn't focus on one specific area that needed attention. No, I was working hard and cleaning tirelessly, but my efforts were random and disorganized, leading to my house also being random and disorganized.

When you are starting on this journey of cleaning your "mental house," don't make one thousand goals about how you're going to overcome all the negative things that are permeating your life (Revelation 21:7). Your house will stay cluttered, and you'll end every day dragging your feet to the bed, wondering how you've been defeated again. This book is to help you pinpoint how FEAR is consuming you, then work to polish that single point until it glows and shines. Clean the fridge, then congratulate yourself on how nice the eggs look on that gleaming glass shelf. Sweep the floor, then admire and walk with your bare feet completely crumb-free. Get those dishes nice and sudsy, hey, even hum a little tune while you wash, then compliment that sink on its polished appearance. Look at that! Your kitchen is clean! Even though the rest of the house may need some more work, relish in the fact that you have made it this far (2 Nephi 28:30). Then, rest.

While I do appreciate the importance of a clean house, I value more a clear mind.

The Drop in a Bucket Mentality

Joseph B. Wirthlin said, "I know that each of us has much to do. Sometimes, we feel overwhelmed by the tasks we face. But if we keep our priorities in order, we can accomplish all that we should. We can endure to the end regardless of temptations, problems, and challenges."

Even though I'm working hard to clean my mental house, I find myself wondering if I'm changing fast enough to make a difference. What cadence do I need to follow? Am I on track to be a good disciple? I learned this lesson from one of the most important people to me in my life: my grandpa.

I remember one dry summer day holding a piece of wheat between my teeth, ambling down the dusty road in my duct-taped boots. Even early in the morning, I could tell it was going to be hot. Grandpa, with his big hands and oil-stained shirt, beckoned me to help fix some of the farm equipment that inevitably fizzled out in the July heat.

I had a lot on my mind those days (1 Chronicles 28:9). I thought about college sometimes, where I would go, and who I could become. Sometimes, I felt so tiny, like the monarch caterpillars chewing on their milkweed, wondering if they would ever sprout wings and fly.

The farmyard was littered with interesting buildings from nearly 200 years before. Old horse harnesses hung like skeletons on their aging hooks, whispering of a time long gone. I passed the branding chute, crawled in between the rungs of a weather-beaten fence, and rounded the corner to find my grandfather.

K. Wells is a big man. When he served a mission for the Church of Jesus Christ of Latter-Day Saints, the Native Americans in New Mexico called him Brother John Wayne. My grandpa has lived in Oakley, Idaho since he was little. Everyone knew him, and everyone loved him. When he was a young man, religion was not much of a priority, but he had a desire to find someone who could teach his children to love Jesus Christ. That's when he met Carol Burton. She was spunky and knew horses even better than people.

Her radiant smile was intoxicating, and K couldn't help but come back again and again to see her, even when he went off to college.

They married young, my grandma being only 18. Grandpa woke daily at 3:30 in the morning to milk cows. His beloved bride always followed him, gently holding her pregnant belly to accompany him. He was a poor man, that young farmer. K Wells toiled day in and day out to take care of his growing family. Never had so much of the universe seemed to rest on his shoulders. Those were harder times when a man could work tirelessly day in and day out to earn only a couple of meager dollars.

But it was the light of the dawn that kept his heart beating. The sun rose in the morning long after they did. Eyes crinkling at the braying livestock, K always smiled. Their first child was born, then another, and another. Days were long, years short. Cows were milked, alfalfa harvested, and children were sent off to school.

The farmer grew old in years. Some of his children returned, others kept their distance. K's grandchildren explored his father's land as he explained the origin of sego lilies and dug up hidden arrowheads along the trail. Faithfully, K. attended church every Sunday, served in the temple, and visited others, providing them with the friend they so desperately needed.

When I accompanied my Grandpa to work, I didn't do much. Grandpa called out for a wrench, so I handed him a rusty tool. When he needed a large screw, I would search until I found it. And so it went until we finished the job, me handing, holding, and sitting while Grandpa used his magic to revive the old farm equipment.

On this blistering summer day, I noticed a peeling milk can across the barn from me. In my boredom, I stared blankly at it, mesmerized by the steady drip, drip, drip of water into the bucket.

Where did the water come from? In Idaho, water is scarce in the summertime, usually stored in irrigation ponds. Rain comes infrequently, if at all, and hungry crops beg desperately for that cool relief.

Yet somehow, a bit of life had nestled its way into the ancient shack. The holes worn into the metal couldn't contain the water inside. I didn't think much of it then because it seemed so insignificant. A word from my grandpa snapped me back to the task at hand.

I never thought much about that day with the milk can and my grandpa... until he disappeared.

"Cancer." Hissed the wind, carrying its ugly message across time and reason. I couldn't fathom it. I slumped on my lumpy bed in a humid apartment in Ecuador, tears sliding down my cheeks. I pictured my grandpa in a hospital bed, pale and dying. Agony clawed at my chest, so I crawled to my bedside and pleaded with God to spare him.

Looking at it now, I think back to that day on the farm with the steady patter of water into the milk pail. Drip. Drip. Drip. It's a melody to me, a healing balm for my crumpled spirit (Jeremiah 8:22).

When I look at myself, I see a million things I have to be. My thoughts are venomous bites, snapping down on my arms, head, and feet until I am only the poison. The future looms over me, and the past growls behind me. Despair falls in a chilling downpour from the sky, washing out my thoughts and leaving me with only emptiness (Job 6:2, Psalm 13:1-6).

Then I think of my grandpa. Drip. Drip. Drip. What did he do when the farm neared collapse? Drip. Drip. Drip. What did he do when he struggled to make ends meet to feed eight hungry children? Drip. Drip. Drip. When the school called, when a neighbor begged, or a child cried. Drip. Drip. Drip. Grandpa K. was steady as time itself. Maybe he, too, felt like me sometimes, weighed down by worry and paralyzed with fear.

It was the drop in the bucket that filled his reality, the notion of a better tomorrow that bolstered his hope. Do you realize how many buckets you are waiting to fill at this very second?

Isaiah 64:4, "For since the beginning of the world men have not seen, nor perceived by ear, neither hath eye seen, O god, beside thee, what he hath prepared for him that waiteth on thee."

When you feel tempted to visit the past, let it be. When your brain is racked with solitude as you face an uncertain future, give it to Christ. It is an art to recognize the good you are doing.

Your drop in the bucket matters.

Contemplation: What have you done today? Do you see God working miracles on your behalf? Ponder on the good things and give yourself a mental high five for how great you are!

Faith over Fear

1 Chronicles 28:20 says, "Be strong and of good courage… fear not, nor be dismayed: for the Lord God, even my God, will be with thee; he will not fail thee, nor forsake thee, until thou hast finished all the work of for the service of the house of the Lord."

Deciding to look at the positive side sucks. It's so much easier to absorb the bad because that's what you've conditioned yourself to do. It's hard to take that rest from your mental battle.

It takes courage to be faithful. Faith takes conscious effort, and it most definitely is a choice. Just like you choose whether to have Taco Bell or Dairy Queen, you often decide on faith or fear without even recognising it, and we're too harsh on people who choose fear.

Thomas was afraid to believe his master rose again, so we call him doubting Thomas (John 20:24-25). Peter walked on water and fell, but he still *walked on water* (Matthew 14:28-31). Have you ever done that? In the Book of Mormon, a lawyer named Zeezrom, full of fear and misunderstanding, belittled two prophets of God (Alma 11:21-46). Later, he repented and saved thousands by his words.

Your fear doesn't take you out of God's plan. In fact, it integrates you back into it.

Fear and faith should not coexist together, but they still do. We have to understand that fear and faith are not all-or-nothing principles. They are on a spectrum, pushing and pulling back and forth. There are moments when the faith is stronger and others when the doubt prevails. But do not doubt your personal value to God when those doubts are the leading force. There is a light up ahead. Keep driving.

The Light Will Always Come

"Wherefore, be of good cheer, and do not fear, for I the Lord am with you, and will stand by you; and ye shall bear record of me, even Jesus Christ, that I am the Son of the living God, that I was, that I am, and that I am to come." - Doctrine and Covenants 68:6

When Lindsay Davis and her friends agreed to make a cross-country trip to Ireland, she never felt more excited in her life, even after being nominated as the designated driver. Lindsay loved how the mossy green fields of Ireland contrasted with the shepherds chasing after their flocks and the salty breeze tousling her hair.

What an amazing journey! Every day was full of adventure and fun... until it was time to make the trip home. At four in the morning, Lindsay gripped the steering wheel like a child clinging to its mother after a bad dream. A dark, empty road dismally greeted her while all of her other six friends dozed off before their long flight (Isaiah 60:2). Rain pelted the car as Lindsay peered through the churning windshield wipers, her anxiety growing by the minute. The lives of her friends could be at stake..and they didn't even know it.

Breathing raggedly, Lindsay knew she couldn't stop, or they would miss their flight. In her mind, she began to cry out a prayer. She was terrified. She didn't know what to do.

When it seemed Lindsay reached the end of her frayed rope, suddenly, a row of lamp posts illuminated the night sky. They came out of nowhere after miles and miles of driving through the unceasing storm. God heard her prayers! Light illuminated the way (Luke 1:79).

However, just as Lindsay began to build her confidence, the lamp posts disappeared, cloaking the rental car in darkness. But Lindsay continued to beg for God to send her light again, and for the remainder of the trip, every time she felt she could go no further, a sliver of illumination would light the way once more. [6]

Sometimes, as you strive to change and develop your mind into a more positive setup, you'll hit some dark patches. As thoughts of defeat sneak past your defenses, you may cry out to God just as Lindsay did, asking for a light to guide you through (2 Nephi 2:15). Resting your body does not always mean your mind will pause its frantic pacing. There's a real enemy out there, and he will stop at nothing to break you to his will. It may not come exactly when you want, but the light will come. It is the Son. The Lord understands us. When we feel that our faith is insufficient, he answers us with these comforting words, "Fear not ye: for I know that ye seek Jesus."

Protecting Your Heart

Light and darkness are polar opposites. It is easy to distinguish the difference between the two. What about positive qualities? For example, being loving or kind? Is it possible to take even good things too far (Philipians 4:4-5)? Yes, that caring can be taken to the extreme, to the point where not only do we care, but we *obsess*. In the past, I studied for an exam until my brain split. Then I aced it and cried afterward because I knew there were more tests awaiting me. There was no joy in that moment of triumph. The victory tasted bland against my lips (Hebrew 6:4-5). Sometimes I have a hard time enjoying life because I feel trapped! I'm so terrified of failure, but my mind does not have the capacity to release the idea from my consciousness. It's antifreeze down my throat, but I keep drinking.

A what-if can also have a dual meaning. What if I make a dumb comment in front of my friends? What if I get hit by a car? What if that guy comes and asks me out on a date? Everyone hears the tantalizing whisper of the what-if monster, but maybe it's time to turn those what-ifs into so-what's. Did you know that the number one cause of right-sided heart failure is left-sided heart failure? There are various things that cause this destructive disease. The principal reason is that pooled blood becomes too much for the ventricles to handle. Blood is not meant to stagnate in the body. It must constantly return to the lungs to receive more oxygen and keep the body alive. For a while, the powerful heart can take the backup, but with time, the left-sided failure leads to an excess of blood backing up into the lungs. The right side of the heart, which forces blood to the lungs, struggles to keep up and, with time, weakens and then loses steam. The lungs become stiff, and the rest of the body battles to survive with the lack of oxygen-packed blood. Pressure increases in the veins and arteries throughout the body, shooting water into the tissues. We strain to keep going, but the stronger side of our hearts has already been expanded. Our body gives into the sheer weight of survival, and in an instant, we collapse. [7]A similar mechanism runs our souls. We can become burdened (Psalm 55:22), heavy laden (Matthew 11:28-30), and emotionally weary. Though we have an infinite capacity to fulfill, it's impossible to complete that capacity now. God has given us mortal bodies that tire and wear down. Our spirits sag with the weight of the lives we carry. We drag them behind us, our duties, debts, and deadlines, all making every step heavier and harder to manage. Our spirits, like our hearts, begin to weaken. We can not take on the world. Not on our own. An interesting concept about our spirits is that they were never created to lift by themselves. The infinite capacity of our spirits comes with the fact that we were created to be intertwined with the souls of others. Do you think you're imperfect? Guess what? So do I. You think you are beyond repair. So does he. You can not do this alone because you were never created to do so! The heaviness of the world is too much to bear alone. Our Savior himself asks us to take the arm of the person next to us and leave all of our burdens at his feet. The chains we carry do not need to plague us anymore. OUR hearts will not fail us because we are tethered to something stronger than steel.

Activity: Think of someone else you know who may be struggling right now. If you don't know of someone, ask God to help you find someone to help. Send them a text message telling them you're thinking of them, give them a phone call, or even stop by their house. There is strength in numbers. If you are suffering, there is a high likelihood that someone else is, too.

Duty Words

Even when I knew I was not alone, there were still many grueling days. Habits are tricky to crack. I remember, at one particularly dark moment, staring at myself in the mirror. There were a lot of things on my plate. I was the president of many different organizations, and so many people were relying on me to carry them to victory. At the same time, I was studying academically and running competitive track and field. I felt like a fraud (Proverbs 25:14). Though I was all smiles on the outside, on the inside, I was a torrent of hail, coming down so hard and so thick as to damage all that was inside of me. I stared at myself in the mirror that day, tears streaming down my face. No one knew I was crying, of course. I had to be strong. I felt so alone.

Is this not Satan's ultimate plan for all of us? He wants you to be isolated from the world. Every time you say to yourself, "I have to brave this path alone," he tugs at that loose string on your sweater, unraveling it a little more.

Look at the trend in my words.

Have to.

Need to.

When I see those words now, my heart constricts. These are fear words and duty words. If you let these duty words run your life, you will never, ever be happy. Sure, there are times and occasions for responsibility. When I allow stress to run over my life, I am not happy (Mormon 9:14). I lash out at other people. I feel irritated because I have so much to do. I feel helpless. I cry when I'm alone. But I don't need to stay this way.

Our Savior, Jesus Christ, provided a way to escape. When he was on the road to Capernaum, he called out to those along the way. He healed them; he saved them (Matthew 8:1-3). What hope did they have left in life? They were crippled, blinded, and unseen (Mark 10:47-52). Maybe you feel the same way. We can not always see our wounds. Christ was a good doctor. In the medical field, there is a difference between "signs" and "symptoms." Signs are measurable, such as a fever, blood pressure, or heart rate. More difficult to understand are the symptoms and what the patient is undergoing. This could be something like chills, headaches, nausea, etc. Though a nurse can write down all of these symptoms, she herself can not feel them. She must take the patient's word, and this is often why it is so difficult to diagnose patients with various symptoms but few signs. The Messiah did not need obvious signs to know what his patients needed. He knows what you need, though oftentimes it may not seem apparent to you (Mark 8:1-9). Though we may have difficulty reading the hearts of those around us, the Savior of mankind does not. There is freedom in letting go of the things we feel we have to do.

Freedom is recognizing that you were meant to love your life here on earth, not endure it. Try doing things because you want to, not because you have to. Still not sure if you feel motivated to do so? Change your mindset. The mind is the most powerful mechanism for change. If you're tired, take a break. You are not a failure to recognising you are human. The world will not end if you stop to breathe, to think, to feel. Your soul is precious.

You yourself can never be a failure. Life itself is a success. You are a product of this success. Jesus Christ championed over death (Helaman 14:15-17). Greatness is not within you. Greatness is you! You are a miracle!

Activity: Write down what things you feel like you "need to do" or "have to do" right now. Are they really necessary? Do you really **need** to do these things? What will happen if you don't?

Think hard. What are the most important things to you on this list?
Do you feel happy when you are doing them?

_____

_____

_____

_____

_____

_____

_____

_____

Hope

Satan creates duty words in our minds to erase hope. He is a cackling, conniving presence, always plotting on how he can make your life miserable. The quickest way to break a man's back is to steal his will to live. How does he do that? Simple. Satan goes after your hope (Moroni 7:40-41).

You learn some very interesting lessons at twenty-one years old, and one of the greatest ones that I know is that hope is like a chicken. It starts with an egg, growing and developing, though it's difficult to weigh the progress. When it hatches, it is a bundle of downy feathers. It follows its mother, peeping and scratching along the way. Most chickens spend their entire lives within an enclosure. Some think this is inhumane, but chickens are safest within a coop. I grew up on a farm teeming with life. When a person decides to embark on the journey of raising chickens, they discover that many animals think the feathered fellows are a tasty snack. When I was little, I accidentally cracked the wired coop door open, and an auburn fowl escaped. Within seconds, our dog clamped the chicken in its jaws, whipping it back and forth until it was dead. I was traumatized. I stared at its glassy eyes until my mom told me to stop being weird. The dead bird landed in the trash can where the dog couldn't continue to mangle it.

I am a student of the chicken. They're pretty simple creatures, but they provide so much value. Day after after day, they lay one or two eggs. They're round and perfect, and the best part is they produce more chickens!

But not my chicken. As soon as I released it, the outside world immediately snuffed it out. Creatures beyond the coop are not friendly to free chickens.

Hope is similar (Psalm 130:5). A small ball of light grows within the individual. It may not even be a complete idea yet, but the feeling is always the same. Beaming, illumination of the heart. When it hatches, that hope grows big enough until it can breed more hope unless we snuff it out. The world can be cruel like that. Satan's fingers are in everything, and his greatest wish is to destroy all hope.

A world without chickens. No eggs. No chicks.

Fyodor Dostoevsky summed it up beautifully, "To live without hope is to cease to live."

You may wonder sometimes if you are a hopeless cause. It may be that you are again wrapped in a blanket, stress-eating Doritos, or crying over a demon you thought you had already conquered. You may feel defenseless and scared because you cannot seem to overcome yourself. The bad parts keep popping up. Is there hope for you (Moroni 8:26, Romans 15:4)?

To this, I reply, shut the chicken coop door. Satan is stealing your chickens, one by one. A dead chicken does not produce more eggs.

Hope has won wars and destroyed oppression. Some have nothing to eat at night but wish for a better tomorrow. Hope fills their stomachs when their mouths have nothing to chew. Hope encourages men and women to stand up for what they believe in, even at the risk of their own lives.

Ether 12:4 says, "Wherefore, whoso believeth in God might with surety hope for a better world, yea, even a place at the right hand of God, which hope cometh of faith, maketh an anchor to the souls of men, which would make them sure and steadfast, always abounding in good works, being led to glorify God."

God made the chickens. The chickens make the eggs. The eggs create more chickens. The hope that you feel is not an apparition! Don't push it away! Don't let it fall into Satan's hands. Hold onto that hope (Hebrews 6:17-18). It is hope that breeds the desire to finish the great race that God has put before us. Don't give up hope for yourself.

The Value of Rest…

Now we come to the grand finale of the chapter: rest. Hope is a beautiful gift bestowed upon us by a loving Heavenly Father. But in order to feel that hope again, we must take a moment to pause and rest.

Olympic athletes train for hours a day. Alisson Felix, who represented the United States in five Olympic games, has 11 Olympic medals: seven gold, three silver, and one bronze. She followed a carefully crafted training regimen for her entire running career. At thirty-five years old, she completed her career. Before every workout, Alisson stretched for several minutes, warming her muscles up and then allowing them to cool down again. It is absolutely necessary that athletes allow their bodies to rest; otherwise, they would risk a season-ending injury.

"I think when I was younger, I always felt like I wanted to do as much as I could — quantity was everything — and now that I'm older, and as a mom, it's really quality over quantity," Felix told *Woman's Day*. "It's about training smarter. For me, being able to focus on recovery allows me to come back and get quality work the next day as well." [7]

The importance of recovery can not be overstated. There are times to give everything to push ourselves to the breaking point, but physically and mentally, we as human beings will never be able to keep up with such a grueling schedule. Our spirits will break down and crack, and we will feel weaker than ever before. Pushing ourselves to such extremes will only cause our own hurt, which can set us back a bit in our spiritual progression

When you begin to institute the tactics written in this book, avoid the desire to catastrophize your situation. In my personal experience, it's easy for me to ward off negative thoughts when they come one at a time or when one less-than-ideal experience occurs in my life. It's the unexpected things that trigger my overreaction, the things that I can't prepare for or control. They consume me, and before long, spider webs of disaster play out like a movie in my brain. Because I wrecked my car, that means I'm going to fail my classes because I can't drive. I can't focus, so I can't reach out to minister to new people. If I can't minister to new people, I will die alone. I'm not good enough. I'm not smart enough. This is the end of existence. Thoughts race in every direction, like kids playing red light green light, tripping over each other and laughing, trying to see which one will kill me first. Now, maybe this seems a bit extreme (and for this book's purposes, it probably is), but the point is that when you feel overwhelmed with the past or the future, it's time to take a trip to the present, right here, right now.

NOW: Who are you right now in this moment? Stop to breathe. If you can do nothing else, focus on taking one breath in and one breath out. If you feel frantic, make yourself stop, even if it is only for a moment. Allow your mind to settle into Christ's love.

Sources

1) Johnson, A. (2019). *Finding Joy in Yourself*. Churchofjesuschrist.org. https://www.churchofjesuschrist.org/study/liahona/2019/08/digital-only-young-adults/finding-joy-in-yourself?lang=eng

2) Nast, C. (2022, December 22). *What Does It Mean to Really, Truly Rest?* SELF. https://www.self.com/story/what-does-rest-mean

3) Christofferson, D. T. (2016, July). *Fathers*. Www.churchofjesuschrist.org. https://www.churchofjesuschrist.org/study/ensign/2016/05/sunday-morning-session/fathers?lang=eng

4) Holland, J. R. (2024). *The Ministry of Angels*. Churchofjesuschrist.org. https://www.churchofjesuschrist.org/study/ensign/2008/11/the-ministry-of-angels?lang=eng

5) Dunn, M. A. (2021, October). *One Percent Better*. Www.churchofjesuschrist.org. https://www.churchofjesuschrist.org/study/general-conference/2021/10/54dunn?lang=eng

6) Wirthlin, J. B. (1990, October). *The Straight and Narrow Way*. Www.churchofjesuschrist.org. https://www.churchofjesuschrist.org/study/general-conference/1990/10/the-straight-and-narrow-way?lang=eng

7) US Olympic Committee. (n.d.). *Allyson Felix Biography, Olympic Medals, Records and Age*. Olympics.com. https://olympics.com/en/athletes/allyson-felix

CHAPTER 3: RESISTANCE, RESILIENCE, RELAPSE

When I first recognized how often I hid behind a mask, I writhed against the thought. My mind gave me all sorts of excuses as to why I had always been happy. People commented that I was always a bright ray of sunshine (Isaiah 29:15, 2 Nephi 27:27). I received awards and praise for all of the hard work I put into my life, and yet, if I dug down beneath my own persona that I assumed, the foundation crumbled on sandy ground (Matthew 7:26, 3 Nephi 14:26). The concrete forms were shifting and cracking, and my house began to warp on its footing, but still, I fought back. Even when I recognised how miserable I was, it seemed almost impossible to change. I simply didn't know how to do it. I cried out to God in the mornings, asking for help. I studied my scriptures and sometimes had small breakthroughs, but still, I wasn't sure how to continue. How could I change the person that I had always been? I didn't know how. Sometimes I didn't want to. I wished my fantasy life could only be true, that deep down, I didn't worry I would end up living in a garbage can because I couldn't get a degree. When I finally took my first step forward, it was deciding that I would not cry after I got done with exams. Exams were very difficult for me in college. Because I received straight A's in high school, I held myself to that same standard at my university. I obsessed over it, pouring myself into studying day in and day out. I worked incredibly hard because I knew what my goal was. Inevitably, after receiving a good grade, the pressurized dam of emotions would break loose. Tears would break loose. I'd cry and cry and tell myself to be happy, but I just couldn't. I didn't feel happy.

When I began writing this book, I realized that I needed to adjust my mindset. My unhappiness was compounded by my incredibly low self-esteem. I was stressed because I didn't believe I was capable of succeeding. I saw myself in the mirror, and the constant battery of words collided against me: "Your skin is so dry." "What an idiot." "You never do anything right."

My constant conversation with myself was about how terrible I was and how I needed to push myself to the very limit to be able to reach success.

So, I decided I wanted to change. I started reading books and listening to podcasts. I focused on telling myself how talented I was, how pretty I was, and how I was going to be okay. Many times, the words clicked. My smile radiated a real joy, one that only emerges from a belief that God trusted me and wanted me (Alma 19:13, Doctrine and Covenants 35:21).

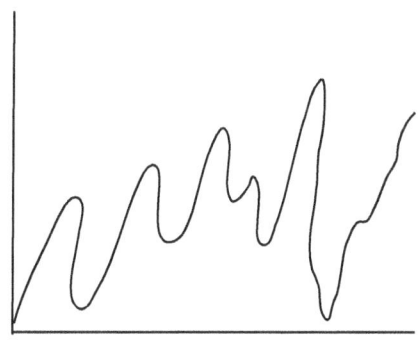

Then came the relapse. Breathlessly falling from the spiritual high back into the same bad habits. Fear has a way of constricting everything, stealing the joy away. In the world of drug rehabilitation, recovering addicts are told to be easy on themselves and not give up if they fall back into old habits. Relapse, remit, relapse, remit. One thought would needle its way into my brain, and I would shove it out, remind it of its place, of how it didn't belong there. Then, another thought would manifest – stronger, sharper (Acts 8:23). That's how I would describe it: a slicing pain, the kind that splits your skin in two and leaves you reeling at the damage it made. Maybe I wasn't good enough. After all, if I had another thought like that, maybe that's what I truly was. As soon as I gave in, the floodgates wooshed open, and I was engulfed in a hurricane of attacks (Helaman 3:29).

I was impressed by the story of a young singer named Nightbirde. She worked nearly her whole life to enter the big stages of the music world. When Nightbirde was young, she wrote her own songs, dreaming of the day she would be able to make a difference. In her lifetime, this brave young woman was diagnosed with cancer three times. Three cancer relapses. Nightbirde wrestled before the Lord many times, writhing in her own pain and begging him to take it away (Psalm 88:1, Habakkuk 1:2). Recently, the brave woman succumbed to her illness, but not without leaving one last memoir to the God who rescued her from the bitterness of her own heart. Here are her words: [1]

"I don't remember most of Autumn because I lost my mind late in the summer, and for a long time after that, I wasn't in my body. I was a lightbulb buzzing somewhere far.

After the doctor told me I was dying, and after the man I married said he didn't love me anymore, I chased a miracle in California, and sixteen weeks later, I got it. The cancer was gone. But when my brain caught up with it all, something broke. I later found out that all the tragedy at once had caused physical head trauma, and my brain was sending false signals of excruciating pain and panic.

I spent three months propped against the wall. On nights that I could not sleep, I laid in the tub like an insect, staring at my reflection in the shower knob. I vomited until I was hollow. I rolled up under my robe on the tile. The bathroom floor became my place to hide, where I could scream and be ugly, where I could sob and spit and eventually doze off, happy to be asleep, even with my head on the toilet.

I have had cancer three times now, and I have barely passed thirty. There are times when I wonder what I must have done to deserve such a story. I fear sometimes that when I die and meet with God, that He will say I disappointed Him, or offended Him, or failed Him. Maybe He'll say I just never learned the lesson, or that I wasn't grateful enough. But one thing I know for sure is this: He can never say that He did not know me.

I am God's downstairs neighbor, banging on the ceiling with a broomstick. I show up at His door every day. Sometimes with songs, sometimes with curses. Sometimes apologies, gifts, questions, demands. Sometimes, I use my key under the mat to let myself in. Other times, I sulk outside until He opens the door to me Himself.

I have called Him a cheat and a liar, and I meant it. I have told Him I wanted to die, and I meant it. Tears have become the only prayer I know. Prayers roll over my nostrils and drip down my forearms. They fall to the ground as I reach for Him. These are the prayers I repeat night and day; sunrise, sunset.

Call me bitter if you want to—that's fair. Count me among the angry, the cynical, the offended, the hardened. But count me also among the friends of God. For I have seen Him in rare form. I have felt His exhale, laid in His shadow, squinted to read the message He wrote for me in the grout: "I'm sad too."

If an explanation would help, He would write me one—I know it. But maybe an explanation would only start an argument between us—and I don't want to argue with God. I want to lay in a hammock with Him and trace the veins in His arms.

I remind myself that I'm praying to the God who let the Israelites stay lost for decades. They begged to arrive in the Promised Land, but instead He let them wander, answering prayers they didn't pray. For forty years, their shoes didn't wear out. Fire lit their path each night. Every morning, He sent them mercy-bread from heaven.

I look hard for the answers to the prayers that I didn't pray. I look for the mercy-bread that He promised to bake fresh for me each morning. The Israelites called it manna, which means "what is it?"

That's the same question I'm asking—again, and again. There's mercy here somewhere—but what is it? What is it? What is it?

I see mercy in the dusty sunlight that outlines the trees, in my mother's crooked hands, in the blanket my friend left for me, in the harmony of the wind chimes. It's not the mercy that I asked for, but it is mercy nonetheless. And I learn a new prayer: thank you. It's a prayer I don't mean yet, but will repeat until I do.

Call me cursed, call me lost, call me scorned. But that's not all. Call me chosen, blessed, sought-after. Call me the one who God whispers his secrets to. I am the one whose belly is filled with loaves of mercy that were hidden for me.

Even on days when I'm not so sick, sometimes I go lay on the mat in the afternoon light to listen for Him. I know it sounds crazy, and I can't really explain it, but God is in there—even now. I have heard it said that some people can't see God because they won't look low enough, and it's true.

If you can't see him, look lower. God is on the bathroom floor."

It was demoralizing to scramble my way out of my low self-esteem, only to plummet back to what seemed like level zero. My head ached from pushing the negative thoughts away, but they always seemed to find a way to slither back into my mind (Alma 36:16-18). They tasted like a discarded bag of chips. Soapy. Stale. Like the thoughts had been in my mental cupboard for way too long after forgetting to throw them away.

Bob Gardner shared a revolutionary perspective in his podcast *Alive and Free.* When we hear the word relapse, we often think of drugs and alcohol. We see rehab facilities and obliterated lives. Most "addicts" become fixated on relapse. They label themselves as a minute population, the screw-ups, the wasted opportunities. What they do not realize is that words like "addiction," "relapse," and "recovery" are terms our feeble human minds use to contemplate the complexities of life. Suppose someone is fortifying their courage to stop eating so many Twinkies. They go cold turkey after a steady diet of three Twinkies per day. For a while, the determination is strong. Their minds are fortified against the temptation to lean on their favorite gooey yellow treat. Then life happens: the buildup of internal stress causes the body to search for anything to make itself feel better. You start getting angry with people because it momentarily allows you to feel powerful. You might wolf down food to stimulate the nervous system. It doesn't matter what the trigger is; it matters that the action makes you feel good, even if it's only for a moment. Behavior is a sign that your caliber of life has plummeted. We all have ways to cope, but did you know that your thought patterns are a way for your mind to adjust as well? Our bodies are fighting to defend themselves from outer harm. It is a standard adaptation that all creatures have. What we don't realize is that our mind's defense is often self-destructive.

Relapse is detrimental to finding our respite. We define the addict by the regression instead of by their progress. One slip-up, and all of a sudden, they are on ground level again. Your mental health can become like an addiction. Our brains create patterns that make it easier for us to process the universe. We become "addicts" to certain phrases and mindsets. We are drunken on our self-pity and dismay (2 Chronicles 20:15,17). We repeat that we will never forgive that unforgivable person who hurt us. Ever. Then, we inevitably find ourselves trying to change. Stumbling up the face of a rock wall and falling short of the peak. And when we fall? Do we give up? No.

It's time to let go of the labels. Addicts become free when they stop calling themselves addicts. When they fall, they dust off their jeans, clean their wounds, and start walking again. They allow Christ to heal them (1 Peter 2:24). Your destiny is not determined by the falls you take.

When you wonder if it is all worth it, picture visiting your favorite place without anxiety. Picture living each day without fear of a mental breakdown. Don't ignore whatever you did or thought. If you are telling yourself self-destructive things, it's your soul trying to tell you something is holding you in a loop. Get out of the cycle! If you fail, try again! Nobody is tallying up how many times you made a mistake, and if they are, you can tell them to focus on the beam in their own eye.

"There will be times when your strength isn't enough, when you struggle, and relapse, and feel like a total failure. If you base your identity on Him, your performance doesn't have to define who you are anymore. You will know that you are fully adored, and wholly accepted in both good times and bad." -Michael J Heil[2]

I wish to say something about the relapse portion of your journey. For me, the relapse into my old thinking patterns and ways played into my black-and-white thinking. I was either a failure or a success. In my mind, melting into my previous self could only signify failure. I've learned since then that it is not about *when* you change or *how* you change but *why* you change. What is keeping you going? Are you tired of being miserable, exhausted, or stressed? Me too! There's something about life that seems to drag me down sometimes. I choke on my aspirations for greatness, wincing at the blows I administer to my own cheeks. Christ does not want that for me, and He does not want that for you. Your progress matters to God, and so does your effort! Do not discount yourself for one minute!

Faith/Fear Spectrum

On the topic of progress, let's consider faith and fear for a moment here. I've heard thousands of times that fear and faith are opposites, like the yin and yang, one evil and one divine. That always stung for me, a person riddled with uneasiness. Did that make me evil as well? If I had a greater portion of fear in my heart than faith, did that push me over the cliff into Satan's open jaws?

The other day, I watched the physics of a pulley system. It is fascinating how mechanics work and how an individual can haul large objects up a rope using a wheel on an axle. It alters the direction of the force applied. I weigh 120 lbs, and even though I do go to the gym occasionally, there is no way I could lift a heavy 200 lb box to the top of my cabinets (which stand at about 6 feet 5 inches). A pulley stops the bulk of the object from being dragged down by gravity to being lifted up by the individual's effort.

When I'm afraid, I neither increase nor decrease the weight of my load, but I do decrease the strength of my heart. My load seems to increase in density. I question my ability to pull something with so many coffee stains and bullet holes. With faith, my burden does not literally lighten nor laden, it remains the same. When I choose to believe in myself and Jesus Christ, my force increases (Doctrine and Covenants 4:2). I know that while I may not be the strongest, bravest, or prettiest, I can lift what I have been given.

Okay, what about the times that you feel somewhere in between? You know, those immobilizing moments when you are fighting so hard to be faithful, but your rope is wearing thin, and you question if you can hold on anymore or cry out for help.

My friend Tanner has always felt that he was one of these individuals: an in-betweener in a constant battle between faith and fear. His story is one of grit and determination.

The pine tree twinkled brightly in the Hobbs family living room. A roaring fire crackled with the good spirits of the family. Children clutched their gifts in hand, galloping around the house in a make-believe wonderland. Nestled over the mantle was a small wooden nativity set. 5-year-old Tanner Hobbs studied Mary's meek eyes as she lovingly gazed down at the newborn Savior, Joseph tenderly touching her shoulder (Luke 2:7). Even the sheep looked interested in the child lying in the manger (Luke 2:20). Stretching his tiny fingers, he reached for the baby figurine. Even so young, a question burned in Tanner's heart hotter than he could even stand.

"Ok, everybody gather round!" His mom called out cheerfully.

After a few minutes of bringing in the scattered ducklings, everybody settled cross-legged around the tree to give their gift to Jesus. It had been a tradition for years. Every member decided on one goal they wanted to achieve that year for their Savior. It was their "present" to Christ to show their commitment to living his gospel. Tanner snuck out of the room, using the bathroom as an excuse.

Snapping the door shut, Tanner curled his little legs up to his chest. The statue of Jesus haunted him, those expectant blue eyes staring up at him. He yearned to make Christ proud, but to do that, Tanner needed to prove he was worthy.

All he wanted was to overcome all his challenges alone, without God's help (Exodus 18:18). Christmas carols echoed downstairs, a hollow melody that filled the bathroom with a lonely haze. That's how it started.

Years later, Tanner set off to serve a mission for the Church of Jesus Christ of Latter-day Saints. The perfectionism choked down on him like a vine strangling a corn stalk. All he desired to be was God's servant, but every day, he felt less and less worthy to be there. He taught the plan of redemption repeatedly, but could it apply to him?

Tanner sprinted down the track, leaping over hurdle after hurdle, until his foot caught on the bar, and he stumbled to the ground. The rough surface of the track scraped his hands raw, and he questioned if it was even worth finishing the race. Everything. Tanner gave absolutely everything in his soul to serving Jesus Christ (Mosiah 2:20). Then, six months in, his mission president sent him home.

Tanner begged his mission president to let him stay, to let him serve. The questions swirled around him like a dust devil on a New Mexico day. What was Tanner doing wrong? Was there something wrong with him? It didn't make a difference. He was on a flight to Meridian, Idaho, the next week.

At 1 AM, Tanner slammed his fist on his linoleum kitchen table. A spotted border collie paced back and forth outside of the screen door, anxious to give his owner solace. Tanner glared at his mug of water, which read cheerily, "You can do it." Bitterly, Tanner laughed. No, he couldn't (Job 6:2). He was a screw-up. A loser (Psalm 69:20). What did God want from him?

The wintery eyes of the wooden baby Jesus flashed in his mind. The years he gave to Jesus continually fell short. The hours he contemplated the scriptures and dedicated his heart to prayer all added up to nothing. Everything he had volunteered was a waste.

I met Tanner in a small business class in college. He struck me as very genuine and sweet, but the more I speak to people, the more I realize how broken we all truly are (2 Nephi 2:7). He opened up to me about his grappling with his own self-loathing, and I realized in an instant how that small child born in Bethlehem had rescued Tanner from himself.

These are his words:

"I'm used to being picked apart by the people I love most, so to ease my pain, I start ripping myself apart before they can reach me. It hurts less when I shred myself apart. That's where my perfectionism got worse. It stems from a fear of rejection. I've been burned very few times, but it hurt enough to decide I would never let it happen again. Even from the time I was a child, my compulsion was black or white. I'm not perfect, so why would I even start? There's no gray area. It's either I'm perfect, or I'm not.

"When I opened up to my friends about this, they told me how good I am, but I don't have to convince you I'm good, I need to convince *me* that I'm good. I know what I've done better than anyone. I know I am accomplished. I know people love me, but it will never be enough.

"Can I overcome it? Yes and no. Every part of my perfectionism is situational. When it comes to hobbies and interests, I feel a lot more secure about my ability to overcome. If I put in effort, it usually works out.

"Maybe it's because I'm struggling right now; I don't have a lot of hope. In relationships, I self-destruct. In the end, if I get into a relationship or not, it won't solve my perfectionism. When I get into a relationship, all I look for is my expectations. All I want is to be happily married with a family.

"This is one of the hurdles I've had to jump over again and again. I thought I needed other people's experiences to be perfect. Coupled with shallow self-esteem, I craved God's approval. I begged for these big, overwhelming circumstances to happen so that God would reveal how much I mean to him. I remember being angry for most of my mission. I felt like I needed to feel a specific way, and I wasn't feeling it at all! In the end, I came to one point: I need a Savior. I believe that the Book of Mormon is true. Period. My brain gives me ultimatums, so I decided to give myself an ultimatum. I love the doctrine in the Book of Mormon. I love Jesus Christ. I told my brain to stuff it with those two simple declarations.

"Anything that blocks your hope for tomorrow can be erased with Christ. I believe I have a Savior, so that's all I need for now. If I'm going to label myself as a perfectionist, I'm going to label the Book of Mormon as true. There is a gray area. It's called the growing area. You don't have to be perfect now, you have to grow. Christ makes gray area possible (Acts 4:12)."

Christ was a baby born in a manger: unremarkable and wrapped in poverty. But that baby was destined to change the world (Doctrine and Covenants 20:21-24). There are some remarkable people whose legacy lives on even beyond their death. In that way, they follow the Savior. Maybe you, too, have passed much of your life feeling unremarkable. That's where the lesson is to be learned. There is power in being you. Just as Christ lived to fulfill his destiny, you are here to do the same! Greatness can be overwhelming. When so many shortcomings trickle through the fissures of your mind, that future seems impossible to achieve, so take it one day at a time.

Learning to Love the Fall

When I talked to Tanner about the relapse portion of his story, he replied, "You know, it's interesting, I'll be good for a moment, and then I'm not. It's my resting state to return to my perfectionism. It feels like a house of cards that I'm trying to climb. The better I feel the harder the fall is. Let's say I did well on a test or scored while playing volleyball. The higher I climb the more anxious I feel. When I'm confident I'm comfortable, but when I fall I am also comfortable. Even the smallest things can make me fall so hard."

Paul Cohelo once said, "You drown not by falling into a river, but by staying submerged in it."

Rarely do we see falling as a good thing. A child falls and scrapes their knee, or a bird falls from a tree and breaks a wing. We see it from the superficial level of Adam and Eve, who fell a great distance from the presence of God (Genesis 3:22-24). Falling always seems to result in pain.

What we fail to see with our finite minds is the infinite growth that comes from falling. The bird that breaks its wing learns to survive on the ground. The child who scrapes his knee learns where to place his feet. He gains kindness and compassion from those around him. Adam and Eve gained understanding and wisdom that allowed them to be the parents of all the earth (Moses 5:9-13).

Regressing to a self-destructive behavior stings and only worsens with repetition. Perhaps it's for a reason. At some point, we come to recognize the shattering disappointment we have become. It blends into blinding frustration and sleepless nights as we lay awake wondering why we are doing this to ourselves. The freezer may be full of Ben and Jerry's, our wall full of patched holes, or our loved ones full of pity, but we are getting better (2 Peter 3:18).

The anger of falling turns into a grim perseverance towards one goal: to stop. We flounder under our weakness and go through the same cycle one hundred times (Omni 1:26). Does it matter how many times you are gasping for breath or how many times you clutch a tree branch for support? No. It matters that you keep going.

Tanner hasn't overcome his perfectionism. I still have anxiety. Jesus Christ is still perfect. Notice the two changeable things here and the one unfailing counterpart. Jesus Christ doesn't care how many times you feel like a failure. If you tried the same thing one hundred thousand times, he would be there in the race with you to the bitter end (Alma 34:16, Ephesians 2:8).

"For, lo, he that formeth the mountains, and createth the wind, and declareth unto man what is his thought, that maketh the morning darkness, and treadeth upon the high places of the earth, The Lord, the God of hosts, is his name." -Amos 4:13

Throwing Away the Negative

Once we've come to terms with the fact that we're undeniably human, we need to learn a crucial skill: leaving behind negative thought patterns. I learned this lesson from a rock…

A growling white truck bumped alongside my tired legs as I shuffled through a dusty field. Rocks and boulders clanked in the trailer like some kind of primitive jazz band. I begged the churning black clouds to rain so I could rest from this distasteful chore: rock picking.

It happened at least once every year at the tail end of a blustery Idaho winter. Planting season came again, which meant the fields needed to be disked and stripped of large rocks before the crops could be planted. The announcement from my dad always received a series of groanings and complaints, but of course, like good little future farmers of America, we went and did as we were commanded (1 Nephi 3:7).

We clodded up the length of three football fields, bending down and grabbing hulking stones and tossing them into the trailer. It was long, strenuous work that always left our backs aching by the end of the day.

Generally, there was little value held with these sooty boulders, but one day, as we were discarding the rocks in the trailer, my cousin held one up to admire it.

She poked me in the shoulder and said, "Look at this rock, Emree! Isn't it special?"

I turned to peer at it, "Looks like a normal rock to me."

Bumps, edges, grey-brown; it was a pretty standard stone. Despite advice to discard the "special rock," my cousin decided to hold onto it. She carried it for the next several hours of rock picking, then to our house, then to her house! When I visited her for a playdate a couple of weeks later, she had converted all of her American Girl Doll Clothes into rock clothes! She named her prize Claude. Over the years, no matter where they moved, I knew I could always find Claude relaxing reliably on the windowsill. My cousin went to college, and we lost touch for a while, but I came to find out later that Claude had finally been laid to rest in a rock garden when my cousin married her high school sweetheart.

No matter how much we paint or dress it up, a rock is a rock. It isn't a toy. It isn't a paperweight, it is a compressed piece of sand or molten lava. We can call it whatever we want, but a rock will always be a rock. Whether it be a diamond, limestone, or obsidian, a rock is still a rock.

Sometimes in life, we try to hold onto our favorite sins (Mosiah 4:10). We dress them up and name them, saying that someday we will get rid of them, but even when we stop playing with them consistently, we refuse to throw them out completely. Thinking patterns can be the same way.

We can have thinking patterns that are difficult to let go of and that ring incessantly in our ears. Though we may have thought we released them the day before, perhaps they come back the next day! What do we do then? Well, throw it away again (Ether 5:5)!

Every day is a unique experience. Your mentality paints your reality. Some people say they're trying to tackle some problem, and it returned exactly the way it had before. Is it feasible to go back anywhere? Can you completely reconstruct anything? Nope! You can try, but it will never be exactly the same. Your mind undergoes constant change. Each experience is unique (2 Corinthians 5:17). The way to change is to understand every circumstance as unique. Don't try to put a thread through all these different experiences (Revelation 21:5). Stay in the present. Breathe, and remember that it's enough that you changed once. If you could do it once, you can do it again. Your thoughts are not your master. You are.

If you're having a hard time justifying the removal of some behavior or if it seems too hard, ask yourself where you want to end up one year down the road. Is this thought process or behavior helping you towards that goal? If the answer is no, it's time to implement some adjustments.

To help you understand this idea better, I want to introduce you to my friend Suzy.

Suzy is a mind reader. Or so she thinks. Even though she gave her best effort to braid her hair elaborately, she left a couple of bumps in the strands of hair. Her classmates are looking at her, not just looking, but staring at the horrid mess of a hairstyle she concocted. She knows for a fact that they think she is an idiot because she just can't do anything right, least of all her hair.

Because today Suzy's hair was terrible, she begins to think of all her previous bad hair days, how stupid she is, and how everyone in the school must be convinced she doesn't even know what a hairbrush is. In agony, she scolds herself over and over for not doing better, which then flies into how she will never be good enough (1 Chronicles 28:9).

Always and never are dangerous words. I'll always be this way. I'll never get better. I always do this. I'll never do that. It perpetuates a spirit of hopelessness. If Suzy spends her whole life trying to read other's minds, she'll end up letting "Big Meanie" have free rein. Imaginary audience is a phenomenon in which teenagers believe there is someone constantly watching them and assessing their every move. Many psychologists declare this strictly as a youth behavior, but for many, it spills into adulthood, breeding a society of "mind readers," thousands of adults who believe they are under neverending scrutiny. Maybe you've felt this way before. I have!

Suzy is collecting rocks, rocks that are heavy and useless. She dresses them up to say that she's telling herself what everyone around her is probably already saying, but in reality, she's projecting her reasoning onto others. How can she truly know what people are thinking of her? Ask them. But the problem is that even if Suzy did venture to ask someone what they thought of her hairstyling abilities, she wouldn't believe them because she has collected a weighty rhetoric of carefully crafted lies.

Though the obvious answer would be for Suzy to throw away the rocks she is carrying about her self-image and her character, it would be unimaginable for Suzy to discard them all at once. Why? Comfort. Suzy is used to carrying her rocks, and her body is strong enough now to do so, so it will be a struggle at this point to completely do away with every negative thinking pattern at once. The sunrise of change brightens with one rock at a time.

Suzy begins her healing process by telling herself every morning how beautiful her hair is. Though she doesn't necessarily believe it, she says it. Then, she reinforces the statement with how kind she is, how brave she is, and how needed she is. It almost sounds silly, but Suzy drops a stone to the ground. For a long time, Suzy couldn't stand the sight of her hair, no matter what she did. Never enough. By throwing the stone away, she recognized how much lighter her step was without it!

I'm not saying that this theory is a cure-all strategy but a method to constantly progress.

Activity:

Think to yourself something that you say to yourself when you make a mistake. For example, "I'm so dumb." or "I can't get anything right." This is a reaction that stems from a negative thought process about yourself. Why do you think you are dumb in this moment? Don't allow other instances to enter your reasoning. Just now. Remind yourself why you are most certainly not a brainless dummy and toss the idea. If it comes back in the future, don't connect it to your past experience. Repeat this process daily, and with time, try to erase the negative reaction to something along these lines, "Oh well," "I'll get it next time," "This doesn't define me."

Learning to Let Go

Sometimes, even when we are learning to throw away individual thoughts that are untrue or unhelpful, we may still struggle with the big picture.

Now that you can understand the small picture, it's time to turn back to the bigger one. There will be missteps in your course, but the most important thing is that you're turned in the right direction.

I learned this lesson during my summertime visits to Grandma's house.

I run through the brittle twigs, trying not to catch my exposed toes in my pink flip-flops. It's summertime, and we're returning to our secret hideaway. It's not too much of a secret, only a couple hundred feet away from my Grandma's house, but to me, it was magical. My cousins follow behind me, hauling various treasures from the "junkyard" behind my grandpa's house. The trees offer us protection from the outside world, and we enter our little paradise.

A twisting stream bubbles near our feet. We dip our hands in the bank and drink the cool water, giggling at the dirt on our pink cheeks. A magpie glares at me from above as I wriggle my hands in the current, attempting to snag some imaginary fish (Genesis 1:1-26).

We build ships from the bark of the gnarled walnut trees, carving a hole for the sail with a small steak knife we discovered on the side of the road. I love my ship. It is earthy and beautiful, and it easily beats my cousin's vessels and the other boats of my cousins in a race. Placing them in the cool brook, we chase them across the old dirt road and pluck them out of the water again and again. Eventually, we get bored of them, and as young children do, we leave our boats on a stump and run off to our next adventure.

Years later, I returned to our "secret spot." Our precious valuables are gone now, cleared away by others sometime before. Nostalgia films the whole scene in black and white to me now, and I reverently touch the dying trunks of the black walnut trees. I'm much older now, and the world is much more complicated than it used to be. Everything is gone from our fortress, leaving only bird nests and old memories.

But As I sit and listen to the finches chatter, I notice, out of the corner of my eye, an artifact from my past. Quietly, I lift the bark boat from its resting place. The rudimentary shape makes me chuckle, and I turn to face the stream. Part of me longs to hold the vessel close and place it in a box to show my grandchildren, but the craft seems to frown at me, the grooves forming begging eyes.

"I am meant to sail," It cries out to me, "Let me go to the water."

I turn the creation over in my hands, which has been rubbed smooth after years of disuse, "But I will keep you safe," I try to reason with it, "You will float away if I put you in the water."

"Exactly," The boat retorts, "I do not belong with you anymore. Stop holding on."

When you are in the thick of self-reconstruction, some walls will have to come down. It will be painful and dusty. Your inner self may try to cling to some of the remnants of who you once were, just like I wished to hold onto my small ship. But my ship served no purpose to me anymore. It wasn't helpful to my progression, so it needed to be set free. Understand that it is ok to be different than you once were. Every day is a chance for you to become more like Christ, but that will require continual improvement. Letting go is a way to allow new life to blossom in its place.

Reach for God's Light

We learned in the last chapter that God's light will often appear to us when we need it most. But even when the light is right in front of us, we hesitate to reach for it.

In Helaman Chapter Five in the Book of Mormon, two brothers, Nephi and Lehi, journeyed to many different parts of the land, "preaching with great power" (verse 17) and baptizing many unto repentance. Their influence, greatly enhanced by the spirit, reminded the wicked of the truth they had lost. They found Jesus again. But not everyone was so quick to turn to the Lord.

When the two missionaries arrived in Nephi, the land of the Lamanites, angry warriors stripped them of their books of scripture and cast them into prison. Hunger panged in their empty stomachs as mosquitoes devoured their naked bodies. After many days of suffering, guards came to put an end to the prisoners' lives.

As the guards stretched forth their hands to grab the prisoners' ropes, the air burned hot with celestial glory. Fire shrieked down from the heavens, engulfing Nephi and Lehi in its flames. The two siblings, then expecting death by the blows of their captors, looked up in amazement. Their hearts took courage (verse 24), and they began to speak to the men who had beaten them and stripped them of their dignity. What was the first thing they said?

"Fear not…"

But the guards were afraid. They could not help but feel so because they were not surrounded by God-like luster. They were trapped in the dark. Breathing low and fast, they covered their heads to drown out the cataclysmic thickness. The prison trembled so terribly that it threatened to fall, jungle vines tumbling from the ceiling and rats scurrying to safety. "They were overshadowed with a cloud of darkness, and an awful and solemn fear came upon them" (Helaman 5:28). The fear was so potent that all stamina drained from the men. They could not flee because they could not move, except for one. There was a Nephite among the captors, one who had known Jesus Christ (3 Nephi 5:13). Though he strayed, this fallen follower looked to see Nephi and Lehi, who conversed easily with the glowing angels. How he must have longed to be there, to be free of that miserable muck.

"And it came to pass that this man did cry unto the multitude, that they might turn and look. And behold, *there was power given unto them* that they did turn and look; and they did behold the faces of Nephi and Lehi" (Helaman 5:37).

This is what I want to focus on here. You're in the dark. You're lost. You're hurt. You're scared. You're confused. Take your pick of any of these or add your own if you would like. Maybe it all just feels too much. The walls are closing in on you, and the gloom is becoming more than you can bear.

Just look. Alma Chapter 33:22-23 says, ".. Cast about your eyes and begin to believe in the Son of God, that he will come to redeem his people, and that he shall suffer and die to atone for their sins; and that he shall rise again from the dead, which shall bring to pass the resurrection, that all men shall stand before him, to be judged at the last and judgment day, to be judged according to their worlds. And now, my brethren, I desire that ye shall plant this word in your hearts, and as it beginneth to swell, even so, nourish it by your faith. And behold, it will become a tree, spring up in you unto everlasting life. And then may God grant unto you that your burdens may be light, through the joy of his Son. And even all this can ye do if ye will. Amen."

Life can be heavy and dark too often. Fear makes it more so. In Chapter One, you were able to dig down to the roots of your emotions and your feelings. You already have a tree growing in your yard. Some of the roots might be poisoning the branches, but that doesn't mean you should chop them down. God is the master gardener. He planted all of the trees, sycamore, pine, and maple, so you could enjoy their diversity. Don't cut down the tree you have. It is part of your story, of your ecosystem. But the fear that has rooted itself in your life will not allow you to grow any further. It is time to plant a new grove: your sacred grove.

ACTIVITY: Growing your faith in yourself and in Jesus Christ

Step One: Plant the seed… How could you grow your faith in Christ?

Ex: Better understand Christ's mercy

Step Two: Water and sun

Ex: Study the scriptures for one month about mercy

Step Three: Fertilizer

Ex: Thank God for his help in learning his plan for you; continue to study other topics that will help grow your faith

Try it!

He Will Come to You

Even when we are trying our best to turn towards the light, that darkness always has a way of finding us. Don't be afraid. You are never alone (Leviticus 26:12).

Boom! The natural wood walls of the log cabin shuddered in the thunderclap. It sounded as if the whole place might tumble down on top of us. My eyes, heavy with sleep, fluttered open in fear. I crawled closer to my husband. He wrapped me in his arms as we listened to the deafening roar of the elements closing in on our tiny abode. Though I trembled slightly, I knew I was safe with him (Ether 2:24).

Two days before, my family arrived at the sturdy log house to spend a weekend adventure in the Arco mountains. After my sister's and my recent weddings, it had been a while since my family had gathered all together in one place. We maneuvered ATVs up rocky trails and fished the mossy lake near my grandma's place. An overall feeling of love bloomed in the thin air as we all settled down for our last night in the grassy basin.

Then it started to rain, gentle dusting droplets that pattered on the tin roof. We engaged in several mildly competitive games of Uno before deciding to head to bed early that evening.

We all woke to the sudden reverberation of the thunder blasting through the house. As I drifted back into a fitful sleep, one thought crossed my mind, "What about Hyrum?"

Hyrum was three years old at the time. I heard his tiny shriek in the pitch black. The younger children were sleeping in the loft, which could only be entered by ascending a steep ladder. Hyrum only scaled the ladder with a hand at his back as an older sibling followed him slowly. I knew he would attempt to crawl down the ladder on his own to reach my mom, who was sleeping on the first floor. The door next to ours creaked open, and I heard my mom's footsteps stepping up the precarious rungs in the dark. Hyrum cried softly as Mom fumbled for him in the darkness. Sitting at his bedside, she clutched him to her chest as thunder shook again. Every stroke of lightning left the child quivering, but mom sang a quiet melody to him, her voice unknowingly soothing her other kids as well (2 Nephi 4:20-21). Then, when the loudest cracks subsided, she carried Hyrum down the groaning steps to sleep in her bed.

Fear paralysis is a real thing. A crashing, frozen mind delicately suspended by threads of suspense can seem nearly impossible to budge by oneself. My younger brother even contemplated climbing down the ladder himself. It was dangerous.

He could have fallen in the darkness and injured himself. My mom, knowing the thoughts of my brother's heart, met him where he was and made sure he was safe (1 Nephi 22:28).

God knows that sometimes you don't know what to do. Sometimes, when you are in the thick of it, it seems like there is no good solution. When you feel unsafe, he will carry you to a place where you are. This is a scary process! You are creating a new version of you! So fear not; God sent his son to sit with you in the dark.

Commitment

You're leaping into a reality of doing scary things. Congratulations! Now is the time to dig deep and show what you're made of, regardless of the pitfalls and regardless of the fear (Doctrine and Covenants 123:17).

"People who are willing to go after something that has never been done before will often find the energy to act based on a couple of different reasons. The first is, they are stubbornly unwilling to accept the fact that the task is impossible, for whatever reasons. The other is they have no choice but to act.

Frankly, they do not need to be totally successful in the eyes of others. As long as they are continuing to significantly increase their own or the world's knowledge about their passion, they will often stay with it. Think of the researcher whose life is guided by a clear mission of finding a cure for pancreatic cancer. That is not just what she does, it defines who she is. In her mind, every single success she achieves or brick wall she hits has a purpose. Each of those efforts is a step closer to a highly desired goal, which provides great meaning in her life."

"That complete devotion to discovery will sometimes lead to astounding successes and a dramatic change in beliefs. There are inventions or breakthroughs too numerous to count that have resulted from people who have been willing to commit themselves to conquering the impossible. As one example, consider Orville and Wilbur Wright. One hundred years ago, they erased the belief that it is impossible to fly, and that led to conquering the impossibility of breaking the sound barrier, which ultimately led to Neal Armstrong's first steps on the moon (which some conspiracy theorists still believe has never truly been done). We should all be thankful that this kind of committed people exist." - Steve Coats [3]

A son and a father sit down at the breakfast table. The son says to the father, "Dad, I've been learning about commitment versus contribution in school, and I just can't grasp it. Can you help me to understand?"

The father pondered this for a moment and replied, "Son, look at your plate. What do you see?"

"Ham and eggs." Replied the boy.

The father clasped his hands together and stared meaningfully at his son. He replied, "You will be asked in your life many times to contribute to different things. At times, it will be your call to commit."

The boy shook his head in frustration, "But dad, what does that mean?"

"On your plate, you have an example of contribution and commitment. That chicken gave a contribution with its egg. That pig gave his commitment. You will have to decide in life where you must commit yourself. It will take your lifetime to achieve it, but that commitment will end in the highest sacrifice. The highest sacrifices bring the greatest rewards."

Will you go all in or sit on the fence? Will you give up or take the easy path out? If it were a life or death situation, would you throw in the towel then?

Be all in. Own it. Go after what you want. You want to heal! You want peace. How bad do you want this? Dream big. The commitment follows dreams. Do you dream of being free? Of being happy?

Are you interested or committed to achieving your dreams? (Team Fearless) "If you're interested you do what's convenient, if you're committed you'll do whatever it takes. You won't continue to be a victim of your current reality and circumstances. You'll come up with reasons why you can achieve it. If you are committed, you'll figure out how you can achieve those goals and how you must versus why you can't and why you won't."

When it gets hard, remember why you started. [4]

You are surrounded by angels- You are never alone

"There is not one of us but what God's love has been expended upon. There is not one of us that He has not cared for and caressed. There is not one of us that He has not desired to save, and that He has not devised means to save. There is not one of us that He has not given His angels charge concerning. We may be insignificant and contemptible in our own eyes, and in the eyes of others, but the truth remains that we are the children of God, and that He has actually given His angels—invisible beings of power and might—charge concerning us, and they watch over us and have us in their keeping." - President George Q. Cannon

There was a waterlogged fence outside of her house. The sizzling sunlight nearly boiled the gooey green sewage running near the old dirt road. I slicked the sweat back into my ponytail, my greasy hair probably appearing more like a biker's than a missionary's. A starved puppy, his ribs pushing into his mangy skin, strained at his rope, begging for attention. I knew better than to pet him now. The last time I attempted to do so, fleas leaped onto my legs and chowed down on my naked flesh. My companion, a five-foot Colombian with coke bottle glasses, glanced at me as she clanked her fist on the tin door, attempting not to burn her hand in the process.

Music blasted in the house, so we knew she was home. But when we shouted, "BUENAS" in the typical Ecuadorian fashion, all sound ceased. I heard a sniffle through the window, which was actually just a hole in the wall with bars over it. We called out again, praying our friend would answer.

Silence. As we were about to continue down the red silt path, the door creaked open, and we saw the eyes of our friend, who I will call Catalina, come into the crack of the door. I've always had a fascination with eyes. Some call them "the window to the soul." Catalina's were as dark as a cup of hot chocolate left on the counter, tepid and untouched.

"I can't talk right now sisters," She mumbled dejectedly, "You know if my husband comes back..."

She didn't finish her sentence. We knew what would happen. We could see it in the blue, bruised skin on her high cheekbones and the way her lips shuddered. My companion asked if we could pray for Catalina.

The door opened a bit wider, and it was then the full force of heartache rushed at us like the heat of an open oven door. I could feel her pain thicker than the humidity outside. Layers of it radiated off her hands as she quickly beckoned us inside. Her two-year-old babbled happily in his chair, hanging from the concrete ceiling. A large TV played a drawing children's show to keep him entertained. Catalina limped in front of us and sat in a three-legged chair. We perched on the deflated brown couch. The air tingled with some evil force that bathed my heart with fear. Words choked from my tongue, and I attempted to swallow the dryness. Never before had such an intense torture ingurgitated my power and will to teach.

With some effort, I whispered to Catalina, who studied her hands, "Let's pray."

Though I was uncertain how I would do so, I closed my eyes and opened my mouth. The first word I uttered was simply, "Father." The murk dissipated from my body, and I spoke more forcefully, feeling as though hands grasped my shoulders. The prayer escalated in intensity until I felt that the room was filled. I opened my eyes, and it was. Hundreds of spirits surrounded us, echoing my prayer with their solemn support. Tears filled my eyes as I recognised that they were my ancestors before me. My grandmother, Margaret Wells, grinned wryly. My cousin Lucas, who had passed away years before, nodded in my direction. I poured out my conscious thoughts to the Lord on behalf of Catalina. Though I do not know if it made a difference to her, it changed me. On that day, I knew the Lord was well aware of my situation. He sent his messengers to tell me I would not fall.

The Very Difficult Journey

You may, at times, feel that you are walking alone. The craggy path eats blisters into your feet as you climb up the boulders and grip the sagebrush. It's a rocky road to wander. Others are traversing it, too, their own lonely path. Maybe sometimes you think it would be easier to stay the way you were. Change is too difficult, too strenuous. It's better to remain in the valley. Do not fall into those lies.

You were not ok before you started this journey. You probably don't feel like you are ok right now. That insecurity is like taking a binkie from a baby. You want something to calm your cries, so you suck your thumb in hopes of respite.

Don't turn back now. There is something to be said of resilience in your tale. It's time to see things as they truly are.

When it gets hard, remember Moroni 10:23, "And Christ truly said unto our fathers: If ye have faith ye can do all things which are expedient unto me."

Contemplation: How have you improved in your journey towards a healthy mind? Have you fallen backward again? What were you like when you started? Are you better now?

Sources

1) Nightbyrde. (2021, March 9). *God is on the Bathroom Floor*. Nightbirde. https://www.nightbirde.co/blog/2021/9/27/god-is-on-the-bathroom-floor

2) Heil, M. J. (2023). *Pursued*. Kharis Publishing.

3) Coats, S. (2024). *Leading Toward the Impossible: What People Believe Makes a Difference*. I-Lead.com. https://i-lead.com/ila-articles/leading-toward-the-impossible-what-people-believe-makes-a-difference/

4) Team Fearless. (2016). *Are You INTERESTED Or Are You COMMITTED? - John Assaraf*. Www.youtube.com. https://www.youtube.com/watch?v=Nrl0YLC-KtM

CHAPTER 4: REPENTANCE

Portia Nelson's poem caused me to come to one conclusion: change is really hard. We don't like change because it tastes suspiciously like the grape cough syrup our moms shoved down our throats when we were kids. It's going to help us feel better eventually, but that definitely doesn't make it taste any better.

But whether we like it or not, change is inevitable (1 Corinthians 15:51). Whether it be positive or negative, it's not feasible for us to stand still. Our hair will still grey, ideas will form, and our lives will be influenced by outside forces. I saw this firsthand through the birth of a butterfly.

My tiny monarch crackled through its transparent cocoon. In wonder, we clapped in elation as the wet creature crawled from its hiding place. Its wings were a mushy bundle strapped to its back. I wondered for a moment how it would ever leave the ground.

I caught my butterfly when it was a chubby caterpillar munching on milkweed. It wriggled and protested, and I was overjoyed at what I found. For many years, neighbors sprayed the milkweed on the side of our dirt road, and for years after that, butterflies became extinct from our country neighborhood.

My mother insisted that I return the insect to its home outside (she wasn't very fond of bugs), but I protested until she finally gave in to me raising it. I loved my little caterpillar. Every day I nourished him with fresh milkweed. I watched him swell larger and larger until one day I found him hanging upside down. When a monarch caterpillar forms a cocoon, they mold a refuge around them. Inside, they begin to change. Days pass by in that green cocoon. We see nothing of the transformation until the enclosure fades from green to clear. Then, the butterfly emerges.

It took at least another hour for the butterfly's wings to completely dry. I was beyond impatient for my pet to fly, but it seemed content to revel in the victory. It had done it. The alteration was complete.

A melancholy feeling nipped at my heels as we gently toted the butterfly enclosure outside. This was the moment we had waited for. As I unscrewed the lid from the enclosure, the wind brushed the gossamer wings. The butterfly seemed to realize this was its time. It fluttered and danced, fulfilling the destiny designed for its kind. My butterfly flew.

It seems mankind has always been fascinated with the idea of flying. Orville and Wilbur Wright tested the limits of the human mind when they soared upon an enlarged version of a model airplane. Birds glide through the sky and kites catch the cheery breeze. When asked what their superpower may be, it is safe to say a large percentage of people pronounce, "Flight."

But what does it take to be able to fly? Well, for the caterpillar, change (Mosiah 5:7). This adjustment took a radical evolution of mind that completely shaped the butterfly's life forever. It took preparation as well. The insect needed to devour every leaf in sight to even consider undergoing such a big variation.

Eric Roth, the author of the Curious Case of Benjamin Button declared, "For what it's worth: it's never too late or, in my case, too early to be whoever you want to be. There's no time limit, stop whenever you want. You can change or stay the same, there are no rules to this thing. We can make the best or the worst of it. I hope you make the best of it. And I hope you see things that startle you. I hope you feel things you never felt before. I hope you meet people with a different point of view. I hope you live a life you're proud of. If you find that you're not, I hope you have the courage to start all over again."[2]

So few people see repentance for what it really is: change. When faced with the word repentance, the world regards it as a thing of naught, an extremist ideal, a derisive pain (Mosiah 27:29). Many understand it as an annoyance, such as the memory of presenting a broken vase to their mother and receiving a sound beating. To them, repentance equals misery. In the field of mental health, repentance can be a constant worry. "I'm sorry," rings like Big Ben at all hours of the day, plaguing the declarant with near delirium at their personal imperfection. Repentance is not meant to break us down, but to allow us to change as a caterpillar assumes its designed role as a beautiful butterfly.

And as far as your mental health goes, you may see repentance as something shameful, something that you have to hide. That's the fear talking. We've sinned, so it's better to sweep it under the rug and act like nothing has happened. Or maybe you didn't sin, but you definitely have some human frailties. Regardless of the situation, the answer is the same every time: repentance=relief.

I wish to right the wrongs cast upon your mind by the unjust rendering of repentance. President Russell M. Nelson has said, "Nothing is more liberating, more ennobling, or more crucial to our individual progression than is a regular, daily focus on repentance. Repentance is not an event; it is a process. It is the key to happiness and peace of mind. When coupled with faith, repentance opens our access to the power of the Atonement of Jesus Christ."[3]

Liberation? Happiness? That's not how we hear the word repentance in the modern Christian world. What about hell fire and damnation? What about the God who is angry at his disobedient children?

Nelson continued, "True repentance is not an event. It is a never-ending privilege . It is fundamental to progression and having peace of mind, comfort, and joy."

We should be stoked that we get the chance to repent. God chooses to say with a little twinkle in his eye that he will "not remember" the things that you've done in the past if you repent and forsake them (Psalm 25:5-7). God chooses to forget. This doesn't mean the memory of our sins is going to be completely wiped from his mind, but that he will choose not to acknowledge them if we are penitent and submissive.

Doctrine and Covenants 58:42-43 says, "Behold, he who has repented of his sins, the same is forgiven, and I, the Lord, remember them no more.

By this ye may know if a man repenteth of his sins—behold, he will confess them and forsake them."

Why would it matter to God if you've truly let it go or not? God is only concerned about your progress, about your desire to do good. It's not even so much about God forgetting, it's about him washing you clean through the Atonement of Jesus Christ (Ether 12:33). When you are forgiven, God allows you to let go of those things too. Try not to bring back old things that were already resolved by a limitless being. This is the posture, the attitude of repentance.

Repentance is how you live your life. It is the pattern of discipleship. Embrace the Atonement of Jesus Christ. Repentance is joyful. It is this mighty change of heart.

There are certain lies that stand outside of our doors like a trojan horse, and we unknowingly allow them to enter our cities.

1. I can't change.

2. I can handle it.

3. One time won't hurt.

4. It's who I am.

Satan convinces us that our faults determine who we are, but they aren't. This is not who you are. Your first identity is always a son or daughter of God (Romans 8:16-17). Recognize the lies and eliminate them! Rip those phrases out of your mind, because they are only excuses to remain in your unhappiness. We search for external labels to find a place in the world. Throw away the labels. Be aware of your labels. Rip them off. Scrape off the excess. Don't let the labels stay around like a cheap bumper sticker. You're not a sinner. That's not how God sees you. Despite all you have done, when you repent, you become a saint through Jesus Christ (1 Nephi 14:14).

The way that you defeat these lies is by replacing them with truth, your true identity.

Meditation Moment:

Close your eyes and remind yourself that your mistakes do not define you.

You are never too far gone to be saved by Jesus Christ.

You can become better, one day at a time.

I used to think repentance was something you did if you were bad, like some byproduct of the fall of Adam and Eve, but it's not. It's not a remedial, kindergarten-like aspect of the gospel. We're not trying to graduate out of it or get past it. It's not just for sin or huge mistakes either. As has been mentioned in previous chapters, your goal is to get better! That's exactly what Jesus Christ is offering you. Repentance is not just cleaning the Saint. It's changing our very nature. Instead of thinking, "Why can't I stop doing this?" you can think, "What can I do now to become better because of this?" or "How will I deepen my relationship with Jesus Christ because of this?"

Sin and Weakness

There is a difference between sin and weakness, and they require different forms of renewal. Wendy Ulrich explained it this way in her book, Forgiving Ourselves, "Sin is described in the scriptures as willful disobedience or rebellion. Sins are intentional violations of the laws of God and include anything we do to rebel against God, ignore his commandments, believe Satan or other people more than God, or intentionally hurt innocent people."[4]

Despite our best efforts, every man falls short of the glory of God (Romans 3:23). We do things that are selfish or unkind, but because of the Jesus Christ's sacrifice, we are able to repent. Do not mistake what I say here. Repentance is not merely knowing that Christ died for you and continuing on in your self destructive behavior (this includes negative thinking habits). No, repentance includes a penitent heart which realizes its own deception.

Here is a guideline for following the steps of repentance.

1. Recognition- understanding that what you have done was wrong or contrary to God's commandments

2. Remorse- feeling guilt over what you have done

3. Confession- this may be to your safety buddy or other trusted loved one, tell them what you have done with complete honesty

4. Forsaking- committing to not doing that thing again ***note if you do fall captive to that same behavior, no biggie! Start from the process over again!

5. Restitution- apologizing to anyone who you may have hurt through your actions

Once we have asked for God's forgiveness and followed through with these steps, we can also forgive ourselves. We can continue on with our lives, but it's all too common that we try to live on toting the pain behind us.

Ulrich continued with another aspect of human nature than many often confuse with sin: weakness, "Weakness, inherent in mortal condition, includes limitations on endurance, judgement, wisdom, energy, skill, resilience, or physical capacity. Human weakness means we will hurt other people out of ignorance, misunderstanding, or insecurity. Weakness can lead to sin, but weakness in itself is not sin. In fact, God is the author of human weakness, while Satan is the author of sin."

We need to respond to these two aspects of our human frailty in distinct ways. When we willfully rebel against God, we must follow the law of repentance and forgiveness. When we recognize our shortcomings, we humble ourselves and ask for God's strength, or in other words, his grace. It can be confusing to distinguish the two. Sometimes we have fallen to both weakness and sin. What do we do then?

Living with Weakness:

One of the ugly sides of human weakness is that we have no control over the circumstances that occur to us. My sister-in-law Lindsey is an incredible woman. She reads her scriptures and listens to self-help podcasts every day. She sends her wonderful kids off to school in the mornings, and I've never met a better cook.

But despite living a pretty idyllic life, Lindsey has a daughter with an undiagnosed chronic illness.

The aching started when Sydney was pretty young. They've traveled all over the country to discover the root of the issue, but every doctor holds a different answer. Autoimmune disease. Lyme disease. Mal's disease. All of them up to this point have been wrong. Lindsey has spent so many sleepless nights curled up in a hospital chair, wondering if her girl, who is now a blossoming teenager, will ever return to normal.

Lindsay didn't do anything to merit Syndey's misery, but it upon her heavily (Matthew 12:48-50). She felt helpless, and that's when things started to go numb. Lindsay's mind floated away from her body as her heart compartmentalized the hard emotions and stored them in the freezer. The freezer was getting really full.

She noticed it happening more and more, the monotonous numbness buzzing around her. It was the only way to survive, to distract herself. The freezer was starting to overflow with untouched feelings, so every once in a while Lindsay would pull out a past experience and let herself discern it. Ouch. Those things stung to contemplate.

Why so many fears?

Why so many unknowns?

Lindsay related to me this wonderful experience, "When Sydney first got sick, it was hard to have fun. I felt constant worry. I felt hopeless. We did all these tests in the beginning. Then I think, 'Now what?' I have no direction. But you learn to handle it better. You do. You have to feel those feelings to live your life regardless of what may happen next. I learned how to get better at being able to have a good cry when needed, but then thinking, 'What can I control? What are my next action steps?'"

I can't change the circumstances: the vomiting, the sore muscles, or the lack of appetite. I can't magically change her and get her better. The wait is the key, so I allow myself to cry.

"For a full year, I felt nothing, but not for lack of effort. I'm diligent about reading my scriptures and saying prayers morning and night. I was doing those things, the primary answers, but I couldn't help but wonder, 'God where are you? Where is the cure?' In December last year, I was driving home from an appointment, and I passed our church building. It was as if a huge hug wrapped around me."

"I felt so much peace that He was with me and that the relief would come. I didn't get a written prescription projected into my brain, but I did see what needed to happen next in my journey. My spirits were lifted and mentally I felt, 'I can do this.' Even though there are times I still feel unsure, I simply say to God, "Stop me if I'm wrong." Then I weep and feel that same comfort I felt when I passed the church. There are others there who are fighting the fight too. I may be weak, but with God I am strong (2 Corinthians 12:9)."

Weakness requires humility (Jacob 4:7). Humility requires us to come before God with a broken heart and a willing mind (Doctrine and Covenants 59:8). There are too many things that enter our existence which are beyond our control. If you attempt to command them, many times your efforts will fall flat. Challenges are like a herd of wild horses. Some of them will willingly bend to our will. Many may take more time and effort. Others will never yield. In all three cases, we can give our suffering to Christ. That is where you will be safest, regardless of the circumstance. Know that if you hurt someone unintentionally or if you have flaws in your physical or mental endurance, this is not sin. You don't need to repent of it. You need to ask for God's strength to guide you through. Everyone is inadequate in some way (besides Jesus).

Tyron Edwards explained, "The first step to improvement, whether mental, moral, or religious, is to know ourselves - our weaknesses, errors, deficiencies, and sins, that, by divine grace, we may overcome and turn from them all."[5]

It's going to be a process. Every day we make mistakes, many of them unintentional. That's ok! What's not ok is excusing yourself from getting better or belittling yourself because you haven't done enough. There's a divine balance in the business of perfection.

So what do we do when we do rebel against God, when we do stray from what we know if right? Then, it is acceptable to follow the steps of repentance, but remember, it is something we can learn to love, not endure! Focus not so much on what you've done, but how you're getting better. That is the attitude of repentance that will quickly propel you forward to success.

Repentance is about giving (Alma 22:16-18). Giving up your pride. Giving your best. Giving it another go. That's what God wants for you. When his Christ commanded Peter and the fisherman to "cast their nets on the other side," He wasn't helping them catch more fish (John 21:5-7). He was teaching them a lesson. Christ gave them more than they could ever imagine, but it took humility. These men were skilled fishermen, and had spent nearly their whole lives out on the boat, rowing, casting, and drawing in their nets (Matthew 4:18-20). This time, they had been searching for hours with little success. They were ready to drop. Then some stranger on the shore calls out to them that they're doing it all wrong! The audacity!

Your net is in the wrong place right now. It will rarely catch fish where it is. Come to Christ's side of the boat. His side is filled with abundance and joy. With Christ, you'll catch more than fish. You'll be able to grasp the never-ending aspect of your eternal destiny. You are God's children. He has sent Christ to come for you. Please, please, cast your net to Christ's side of the boat.

All Christ is asking you to do is change how you think. The truth is, I wasn't sure how I was going to achieve it. I didn't feel peace. I didn't feel joy. In fact, there were times that the unbearable mental battle settled into a dull ache. Where were my fish? In my mind, I had done everything right for him, but my soul refused to be comforted (Psalm 77:2).

113

Romans 8:38-39 says, "For I am persuaded that neither death, nor life, nor angels nor principalities, nor powers, nor things present, nor things to come, nor height, nor depth, nor any other creature, shall be able to separate us from the love of God, which is in Christ Jesus our Lord."

There is this statue hidden deep in the gardens of BYU Idaho. I remember facing her after one devastating morning of sheer gloom. It was a warm June day, a rarity for Rexburg at this time of year. I sought the greenery and foliage of the trees to hide my ugliness, my tear-stained cheeks and swollen eyes. There were many people that day, apparently as shattered as I was, seeking sanctuary in the trees. An empty table greeted me as a twitterpated squirrel shot back and forth between the warped trunks of the weeping willow trees. How I wished to weep like they did: gracefully, their long leaves cascading to the grass like droplets of water.. When I wept, my whimper seemed like that of a toddler who did not know what they desired: comfort, nourishment, or sleep. It didn't matter because the torment drew on far further than what they expected. Inconsolable. Like a small child I felt nearly inconsolable when I arrived at my secret place.

Then I met her—my statue. I didn't notice her at first in the thick of my panic attack. "Stay calm Emree. Stay calm," I muttered to myself over and over, trying to shake the misery. The statue stared at my struggle, her hollow eyes whispering of some untold heartache as well. But as I looked closer, I noticed her eyes were actually not looking at me—they were looking up. At one point, the sculpture may have been white, but her delicate porcelain skin was now stained from years of mistreatment. Kneeling, the graceful statue poured an invisible substance from a grimy vase. I had seen other figurines in the grove before, but none were so melancholy and identical to my current feeling. Where was she looking? Why did she continue to pour when she knew there was nothing inside of her to offer? Look at her! A discarded remnant of what her artist originally intended for her to be.

Maybe I projected my story on her, but in a flash of inspiration, I realized what she offered from her jar. That statue was presenting herself. And who was she giving herself to? Where was she staring at, with those white lifeless eyes?

In my mind, I saw a white-robed man standing above the depicted woman in the garden, reaching down to touch her dilapidated forehead. I knew that this man, unlike me, could restore the woman to her former state, but he didn't because that is not what the Lamb of God was sent to do. I watched him pull her to her feet and rub away her tears with his thumb. He didn't take away the crevices in her skin; he simply filled them with his love. Christ connected his finger with every fissure, and like the ancient art of Kintsugi, he sealed them with gold. Suddenly, the woman understood her great worth. Before, she blown down by wind, rain, and storm. Every day, hundreds of students passed by her and paid her no mind. Her story was insignificant to them. But to Christ, her story was everything because it was His story too.

Your faults do not disgust the Master. What you give to him can only be you. He doesn't want your house or your retirement plan; he is in "relentless pursuit of *you.*"5 Grace works as a free entity. When you are as the statue, frozen by your past, driven only by the need to feel *something,* pour out your soul to Him. If you haven't felt like praying, simply say in your mind, "Lord, I need your help." And He will come. He always comes.

Stop Putting Yourself Down

It took me some time to recognize my worth in Christ's eyes. Though I've always known I was talented, I've always downplayed my abilities. If someone told me I excelled at something, I quickly said, "Oh, I'm not *that* good. There are much better people than me at this." It was painful for me to take a compliment. I convinced myself that this was humility when really it was just Satan twisting and warping my mind to say, "I'm not good. I will never be good." It came to the point that I had difficulty believing that others could love me, especially my husband and God. I loved both of them immensely, but in my mind, I was incapable of receiving the same love from them. Though their tenderness was manifest to me every day, I told myself that I wasn't worthy of it. Why would they love me? I didn't think I deserved it, because I felt like dirt, completely worthless. In my mind, in order to be worthy of something, you have to be worth the sacrifice, and I simply didn't feel like I was. For someone to send their Only Begotten Son to die for *me* just didn't seem right. Why would Christ endure agony for me? What had I done to deserve it? I mean, I made mistakes all the time and then compounded the fact that I didn't even like myself. It almost seemed like squandering the gift God bestowed upon me, and I felt like my value didn't merit his sacrifice. Nathan, has always had complete faith in me. Patiently, told me it would all work out. Shame is an immensely powerful tool, and it swarmed me. I told myself I didn't deserve my husband, not then, not ever. This is where I was completely wrong. We deserve nothing in this life. We don't deserve those drops of blood dripping off of Christ's furrowed brow as He cried out in agony against the sins of the world. We don't deserve the splinters that tunneled into His back as He dragged His cross through the streets of Jerusalem. Do we deserve the nails driven into the perfect hands of the Lamb of God? He entered like a lamb to the slaughter. Why would Jesus do that for us? What did we do to deserve it?

Doctrine and Covenants 18:10-13 has the answer to this question, "Remember the worth of souls is great in the sight of God; For, behold, the Lord your Redeemer suffered death in the flesh; wherefore he suffered the pain of all men, that all men might repent and come unto him. And he hath risen again from the dead, that he might bring all men unto him, on conditions of repentance. And how great is his joy in the soul that repenteth!"

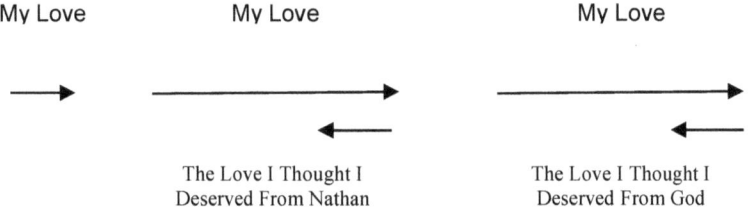

My Love   My Love   My Love

The Love I Thought I Deserved From Nathan   The Love I Thought I Deserved From God

We don't deserve God's grace, but by sending his Son here to die for us, we have been given a free gift: a new start on the conditions of repentance. You can't come back to live with your Father in Heaven again without the enabling power of repentance.

Where do we start?

Activity: Unraveling regret

Regret: From This:

I wish this happened:

If only this:

Why couldn't I have:

To this:

I'm so glad…

I'm so proud…

I learned…

I loved…

Future Fear: From this:

I've always been terrified of_____ happening to me

What if _____?

To this:

I trust that God will protect me or help me to be strong.

I know that God can give me strength to overcome this.

If _____ happens, I know that it will be ok.

When I lived in Ecuador, there was a family of whom I had grown particularly fond. Elizabeth Matamoros jumped between active and inactive for several years, but she loved the missionaries. We visited her and her grandchildren often, teaching them small lessons about the Savior and inviting them to come back to church. Her gray eyes were wise and lined with sorrow. She, like most of us, had endured a difficult life. But she returned many times to that red brick chapel. Elizabeth even became the teacher for our class of investigators, and she found joy in the principles of the gospel again. The night came for me to say goodbye to the Matamoros. My mission had come to an end, and the next day, I would be returning to the United States. We all sat in the ornate living room, beautiful Ecuadorian artwork lining the wall. There was one painting I had always been particularly fond of, and I voiced it out loud on that teary night. It was one of three horses, their elegant heads facing towards an unknown whistle, bright eyes alert. To my surprise, Elizabeth Matamoros approached her wall, plucked the painting off, and placed it in my hands. The painting in Ecuador was worth quite a sum of money. I tried to refuse, but Elizabeth was adamant. She hugged me tightly and said, "If this is the only thing that you can take with you to remember us, please, never forget how much we love you. Come back to us someday."

What has God given us to show that he loves us? His Son. This earth. Our bodies. Our agency. Everything in the universe was created as a manifestation of God's love for us! This is why God allows us to repent.

Laudy Ruth Kaouk observed, "God is cheering for us. He wants us to return to him. He knows us personally. He knows you. He loves us. He is always aware of us and blesses us even when we feel we don't deserve it. He knows what we need and when we need it."[6]

It's not about what we deserve or don't deserve. It's about God giving us a million second chances (to infinity and beyond) (Doctrine and Covenants 101:9). He does it because he loves us, plain and simple. No matter what you have or haven't done, God's love and forgiveness will always be available to you, no matter how far you have fallen.

According to Merrium Webster Dictionary, the word infinite means "endless, inexhaustible, subject to no limitation."[7] You may question when your good fortune will run out. When are your mistakes too much for God to handle (1 John 1:9)? Never. If you ask for forgiveness, you will receive it, plain and simple. There are no boundaries on the devotion of our Father in Heaven (Matthew 18:21-22).

Guilt and Shame

Why do we turn to shame? Guilt is recognizing we did something wrong. We're not proud of what we did, and we feel a need to be better. Shame is when you take those feelings and say that I am bad because I did something bad. Though guilt is inspired by the individual's inner morality, shame stems from their social atmosphere. Shame leads to hiding from your actions. Guilt leads to gradual development. Shame is stagnant. Guilt can grow into an increased sense of self worth, while shame leads to self-loathing and a disfigured identity.

As I have worked on writing the different aspects of this book, I'm often surprised as every week I come across different experiences and people who have helped shape my mental health. The person who started it all for me was my husband Nathan. He's my Superman, but even Superman has his kryptonite.

For the majority of Nathan's life, he relied on shame rather than guilt. He used shame to justify his actions. He'd say, "Oh, look at the horrible things you've done, but it makes sense because you're a horrible person. That's who you are now, and that's who you'll be forever. You can't change it. Well, sucks to suck."

Nathan escaped the shame cycle by telling himself he made a mistake but he's not a bad person. He gets to be a better person tomorrow.

Nathan explained he had the foundations for shame built as a kid. I remember getting sent to time out and thinking, "I'm terrible. I'm awful. My parents don't like me."

Wanting to please his parents made it worse. Nathan strove to be obedient and to be a good boy. That need to please becomes like a shrinking room with no windows or doors. It's a ten-foot hole that you can't climb out of. It's punching yourself in the face and crying out that you want more.. With shame, if it's not one incident that's getting you down, it's always something else. It's a never-ending cycle. Today I feel horrible about this; tomorrow I'll feel awful about that. Nathan felt like he didn't deserve to feel good. For him, a sense of shame should end with a confession or righting wrongs that didn't need to be righted. A constant hungering for redemption gnawed at his spirit (Psalm 111:7-10). Out of the thousands of outlets with which he attempted to escape shame or find a sense of happiness, not a single one prevailed. While many of them provided a short period of pleasure, the feelings of shame always came crawling back.

Why do we continue to run to toxic outlets like pornography, alcohol, drugs, starving ourselves, or excessive working out? Why do we revolve to shame? My husband explained it this way: the feelings of happiness are like a ladder. The first rung is the starting level of happiness, then up to two, three, four, all the way up the ladder. Say you're at a four or five happiness level, and then you start to get stressed and overworked. You feel like you offended somebody or you yelled at your kid. Then you dwell on the past more and more. With all these things piling up in your mind you start sliding down the ladder very quickly. Sometimes you don't even realize it's happening to you. All of a sudden, you're at rung one on the ladder. Once

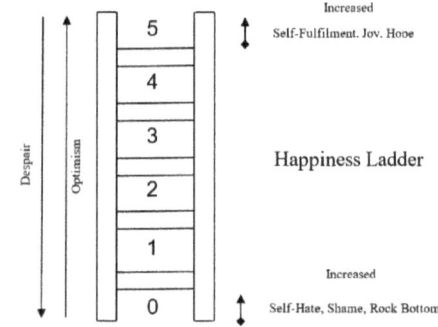

you're at rung one, you're miserable (2 Nephi 2:18). . Your shame increases as you slide down the ladder. You feel so much embarrassment, self-hate, and anguish. You hit rock bottom, and at that point you're comfortable because there's nowhere else to go. You're comfortably miserable because you're used to hating yourself. In a way, you become your toxic best friend. You feel pathetic, but hey, that's normal now. You spin, and you spin because there's nothing else, right?

We all know that there are healthy outlets. We know we should exercise, we should meditate, we know what we *should* do. But we're so low on the ladder, and those things seem really out of reach for our current skillset. They also don't always provide instant release. We're looking to get up the ladder fast. We're miserable. How do we escape quickly? It is easier to fall into negative habits because they're more accessible, and they provide a momentary jump up the ladder. When we make the jump to anything above rock bottom, it feels better than the shame itself. We make a jump to self-harm, driving too fast, sleeping too much, etc., because that's above rock bottom, even if it's only by one rung. They're still more rewarding than where we were at. Then, it becomes the shame cycle. We start cycling between shame and that unhealthy activity: falling and climbing up the ladder.

If you're struggling with alcohol, the problem is not the alcohol, it's the shame. If you are viewing pornography, the images themselves are not the issue, the problem is the shame. You say you're a bad person for doing a bad thing, so you find a way to cope, which inevitably leads back to doing that same negative behavior.

It goes round and round . They make you feel good for a few moments before the consequences sink in, then you crumble back into shame. You may even get out of it for a while. After a few days of doing better, you may say that you're done with your negative coping mechanism forever. You return to healthy habits. You make your declaration that it was the last time. You start reading scriptures again, etc. And then, after a few hours, days, even weeks, shame starts barking. An external event may have happened, and you're feeling stressed again. The next thing you know, you're back at the bottom, you're back in complete mortification mode. You will never stay out of your unhealthy behavior until you address the shame.

How do I tackle this problem? I hate to say it, but it's not the exact same for every person. That's what makes these issues so challenging—everyone is different. If you have a mental health disorder, it can make the problem even harder, but the key to this issue is getting down to the very essence of the humiliation

My Shame

My husband is not only my superman, but also my Yoda for all of my mental health struggles. Because of his many years learning how to cope with his OCD and ADHD, he has quite a few tricks up his sleeve to prevent his mind from spinning out of control.

I personally don't understand why I can't give myself a break. I mean, honestly, if some random person I met on the street did some of the things I did, I'd buy them a Dr. Pepper and tell them they're doing a great job.

But it doesn't feel that way for me. Maybe some of you can relate to the story of my Volkswagen Jetta.

I worked hard for that car. Dang hard. I mentioned in one of the earlier chapters my extreme hyper fixation on maintaining straight A's. That probably spouted from a promise my Dad made me when I was a freshman in high school: if I became the valedictorian of my graduating class, he would buy me a car. When I sat behind the steering wheel of my beat-up family car, I thought, "Oh you're on."

After four years, I was named valedictorian, and my "free-car IOU" was paid in full. The Jetta was the nicest vehicle I had ever driven by far. It had bluetooth connection for my phone, mirrors that alerted me when cars were in my blind spot, and brakes that didn't need to be pushed to the floor to stop. I was in heaven. Even in the Rexburg winter wonderland, I was so careful with my Jetta, so careful that I really didn't even drive that much. I drove when I needed to, and that was good enough for me.

When my husband and I were going to meet with our wedding planner, we decided to take separate vehicles. I should mention my $100 Walmart phone at this point in the story. (It plays a vital role). This unreliable cellular device often decided to face me with a black screen of death when I least expected it, generally when I needed it the most. I stopped at the stop sign outside my apartment, but when I glanced down at my phone for the directions, the dumb thing was darker as a moonless, cloudy night. Growling in frustration, I started to make the left turn to head towards the freeway, tapping impatiently at the device with one hand and making the turn with the other. Two seconds later, my body jarred forward, and I realized with amazement that I had hit a car. A parked car. Tears gushed out of my eyes like I had poked Old Faithful with a pickax. Blubbering, I dialed Nathan's number (my phone decided to work right after I smashed the daylights out of my car) and explained what happened.

"No, no, no." I cried as my fingers grazed the mangled remnants of my beautiful car.

It seems this would have been the end of the story, right? The police came, my car got towed, the owner of the vehicle called, and all was well. Only it wasn't. Though only sympathy oozed out of the mouths of everyone around me, I was dead focused on my error.

"Stupid, stupid, stupid." I berated myself over and over again.

Then I pushed my grief away and refused to acknowledge its presence, willing it to go away and leave me in peace. However, shame is like a debt with high interest, the longer you wait to pay it, the more consequences accumulate.

For nearly four months, I hardly ever drove, and when I did it terrified me. I continued to mock myself for being so childish. It was a parked car. No one was hurt. Plus, the car was totalled, so Nathan and I received a hefty sum of $10,000 for my folly. I was being ridiculous. Everybody drives. Stop being a baby.

I still couldn't quite reason with myself. I told myself I deserved to drive the cheapest car possible, so that's what I purchased for myself. I rarely drove my husband's car, which was even newer and more expensive than the car I lost before. I felt like punishment was the only way to prevent the accident from occurring again.

Over time, my shame morphed into a fear of driving. What if I killed someone next time? What if I ruined my husband's car too? What if I worked hard for something else in life only to destroy it again?

Though time continued to pass, I refused to forgive myself. I couldn't. My debt wasn't paid yet.

I let myself be carried away by the shame cycle. I believed that Christ would forgive anybody else but me. What was there to forgive? Had I committed some great sin or denied the power of my God? Yes and no.

Let me explain how I began my process of healing from my excessive shaming tendencies.

The Life Jacket Analogy

Even the strongest swimmers can drown in a river. Currents, rocks, and unexpected waterfalls can drag the person down until their lungs fill with sand. That's why they recommend you wear a life jacket. Of course most of us don't. Especially when we're older, because we're tough enough to tread water for a few minutes. It's not so much that we're unafraid, but more that we feel we have something to prove.

Our spiritual life jacket comes from the life of Jesus Christ (Isaiah 63:9). But then I remind myself why I don't need his protection (Deuteronomy 8:14). I can tread water. I can do this on my own (Proverbs 1:24). In fact, I don't know that I personally deserve his love. I mean after all that I've done, how could I possibly accept the life jacket from him? My head bobs up and down. My body is made of lead. What have I done? I know I can't touch the bottom without suffocating. I also know I'm not as good of a swimmer as I pretend to be. I debate grabbing onto one of the other people with a life jacket, just for a second. I don't want to drown them or anything, but I also don't love the idea of death.

And so is the situation of someone who refuses to forgive themselves. They're sinking real fast, and they have nothing to keep them afloat.

Let's return to my Jetta story and to my husband Nathan.

We were both churning our arms and legs in the river, but neither of us were making much progress. Nathan tried to beat it on his own for years. Here and there, he may have asked God for help, but in reality he tried to do most of it on his own (2 Nephi 9:28). Nathan continually asked God for forgiveness, but rarely for strength. His divine help came through a friend who recognised that he couldn't work on his homework for hours because his brain was spinning and spinning. She said," Nathan, I think you have ADHD." Nate chewed on that for a while and decided to do something about it. He did a mental health screening, and they came back with results that he had ADHD and OCD. From there, he started to rewire his life. He had great counselors who helped him to see the good he had already accomplished.

Once he started to heal, Nathan solidified his connection with God. He knew how God felt about him (Isaiah 49:13). Before Nathan saw his maker as the never-ending critic signing his name on his ticket to Hell. He hesitated to reach out to Heavenly Father, wondering if God could truly help him. Nathan felt he had screwed up way too many times to merit God's mercy.

Now Nathan knows. I think Elder Kearon interprets it wonderfully.

"Please know that the Savior has descended below all things, even what has happened to you. Because of that, He knows exactly what real terror and shame feels like and how it feels to be abandoned and broken. From the depths of His atoning suffering, the Savior imparts hope you thought was lost forever, strength you believed you could never possess, and healing you couldn't imagine was possible."[7]

Nothing is too hard for the Lord (Genesis 18:14).

So.. what about me? How did I vanquish my shame? Well, I must admit that I'm still a work in progress, but I've come to repeat this conversation with God when shame comes knocking at my door.

"I don't know if I'm good in Your eyes, but I am going to try. Sometimes I am afraid to try again, because I worry it won't be enough (2 Nephi 2:45). There are mistakes I will make that aren't fully fixable in this life. What do I do then? Lord, I will give them to thee. Your grace is perfect. I'm sorry I did this, but I'm grateful that you live. Thank you for living your sinless life to liberate mine."

To be able to accept Christ and who He is, I need to understand the Atonement covers all of the ripples I make in my life. Not just the ones that affect me, not only the big ones or the small ones.

ALL OF THEM. This includes the direct and indirect mistakes. Let the guilt go. (Jeremiah 32:17).

"Jesus doesn't just suffer for big, bad sinners, but He knows the feelings associated with disappointment, the feelings of apprehension, the feelings of fear. He knows how to help us with our feelings of inadequacy. He knows how to help us face and fight our way through abuse. He knows how to help us learn to forgive. And yes, He knows how to forgive our sins.

-Bruce C Hafen

Activity: Shame

Do I have regrets in life? What are they?

_____

_____

_____

_____

_____

Are these regrets still affecting me in some way: in how I act or think?

_____

_____

Am I still punishing myself for the things I have done? How am I punishing myself? (be specific)

_____

_____

_____

How do I cope when I feel stressed? Do I feel ashamed when I cope this way? (note: this does not have to be something serious; it could be something as simple as you binge watch your favorite TV show or distance yourself from others)

_____

_____

_____

_____

_____

What can I do now to let this shame go? (if you can't think of something, ask your safety buddy and God for help)

_____

_____

_____

_____

_____

_____

You may think that your many flaws are distancing you from Jesus Christ, but that could not be farther from the truth. Your flaws are the things that connect you to the master of the universe. It is our fear of calling out to God that pulls us away from the Savior's redeeming light. It's when you fall that you may return to him. Everyone is flawed. Everyone is imperfect. You may have felt alone in that regard before. I know I did. Everyone walked, talked, and thought in their perfect little sphere, leaving me wondering if there was something wrong with me. When you are treading water and wondering how much longer you can stay afloat, you can cry for a life jacket. Christ doesn't want you to Only through accessing his atonement can you find the peace you are seeking, but that begins with you accepting yourself.

Forgiveness

Once we've embraced the idea of forgiving ourselves, it's time to dip our toe into something equally unpleasant but equally rewarding: forgiveness of others.

C.S Lewis remarked, "To be a Christian means to forgive the inexcusable because God has forgiven the inexcusable in you."[8]

God told Peter to forgive seventy times seven (Matthew 18:21-22). That's 490 instances of forgiveness. Perhaps that's not the end of our forgiveness train: scratching tally marks on a chalkboard until our rivals reach their quota. No, God gave the greatest commandment to love Him and to love our neighbors as ourselves (Mark 12:28-24). That includes three people who we're asked to love. God, ourselves, and our neighbors.

We may cry out in indigence when we hear that we are required to forgive everyone. Everyone! What about the neighbor whose dog always leaves a personal gift in our flower bed? What about the time our spouse forgot our birthday (yikes)? There are the more disconcerting things as well.

What about the person who raped us or left us questioning if we wanted to live? What about the bullies and the dictators? What about the people who will never acknowledge that it's their fault that we are emotionally mutilated?

It's not fair that they get it off the hook, not after what they've done (1 Peter 3:17-18).

An example of this forgiveness could be as follows:

When Kristi was ten years old, her parents got divorced. Her father cheated on her mother with another woman and was currently living with her. For years Kristi sobbed as her father tore her and her two sisters away from their mother during his weekend visits. Jake, Kristi's father, began to drink heavily and neglect the care of his children. He broke into the gambling sphere and went from mistress to mistress, rarely noticing his daughters changing from girls to women. As soon as Kristi was out of the house, she refused to see her father again. Then Kristi found her relationship with Jesus Christ. She wanted so badly to forgive her father, but there was this invisible force field that shut her out. After some deliberation, she decided to speak to her mother, Lacy, about it. Lacy had been hurt too, so Kristi thought to find her mom bitter and resentful during the conversation. Lacy was quite the opposite. Some years before, Lacy talked to Jake. Jake was still knee-deep in trouble, but Lacy ceased to see him for his actions and more for his identity: a child of God. It changed everything for her. So it began for Kristi. Whenever she remembered to pray, she petitioned for the power to forgive her father. The answer did not come for a long time. A year passed, and Jake asked to go to lunch with Kristi. Kristi declined. Another six months passed. Jake invited Kristi to his wedding. Kristi declined. So much fury burned hot in her chest from the injustice of a little girl. She didn't want her dad to be happy! He deserved to be miserable like she was!

One day, Kristi opened up her scriptures to Mark 2:17, which reads, "When Jesus heard it, he saith unto them, They that are whole have no need of the physician, but they that are sick: I came not to call the righteous, but sinners to repentance."

The spirit penetrated her heart. Falling back onto her bed, Kristi knew what she needed to do.

It's a matter of adaptation that we don't return to something that injures us without some higher reward in mind. A gazelle doesn't bounce to meet the waiting jaws of a lion or a rabbit into the fox's den, but we are living a higher law- Christ's law. Repentance is acknowledging your own faults, while forgiveness is acknowledging the faults of others. In both, it is necessary to love the offending party (Luke 6:27, Matthew 5:44, 3 Nephi 12:44).

Kristi's heart still wrenched with slight distaste as she punched in her dad's phone number. Even though she was committed to having this conversation, the pain still radiated from many years of unfairness. Jake answered the phone and the words tumbled out of Kristi's mouth, "Dad, I just need to let you know you really hurt me when I was younger," There was some vindication in saying it, but Kristi swallowed her pride. This wasn't about getting even, it was about getting better. She continued, "What you did wasn't ok. I was so young, and I felt like I didn't matter to you. I felt invisible, but I'm trying to heal now, and whether or not you choose to apologize, I am ready to let it go because… I love you." The words choked out of Kristi's throat, and there was silence on the other end of the line. Those three words surprised her because, for years, she never would have believed them. Kristi's life had been altered because of the bad decisions of her father. And yet, by gripping the torment with both hands and refusing to let go, she was only attaching herself further to the pain. Whether or not her father chose to accept her apology, Kristi had taken the first step, she had chosen to forgive.

Forgiveness can be defined as letting go of what we think about the quality of the person or their identity. It's choosing to "look to God and live" instead of holding grudges that fester and burn. If you come unto Christ, he will forgive you of all your trespasses, so he asks in return that you forgive others theirs. This doesn't mean that you condone what they have done. However, it does mean forgiving again and again, even if it seems like you're adding more fuel to the fire. There will be some who you should not even rekindle your relationship with. If you feel this person is continually causing you harm, it may be time to step away from them and allow them a chance to repent.

There is no set time you need to make for yourself in order to forgive. In fact, Sarah Montana shared in her ted talk Why Forgiveness is Worth It that often we "forgive" people too quickly.7 The following reasons may be why..

1) It's the "right thing" to do (good person syndrome)

2) Pressure from friends, loved ones, etc.

3) Many think forgiving quickly will result in a faster healing process

Montana went on to explain that far too often when we forgive, we simply brush away the feelings accompanying this person. We yearn for healing, but we aren't willing to do the work to get there. You will find that a quick, "I forgive you," especially for someone who has repeatedly hurt you, most often is going to impair yourself. Forgiveness is independence, but it comes at a price. And it's not the forgiveness that will save you. It's the glorious power of Jesus Christ.

Where does true forgiveness begin?

You can start by remembering. This is what strikes many as the most painful part. It's much easier to move on and let those wounds remain. When you remember, it's important to feel. It's human nature to bluff our own toughness. We don't want those people to ever get the satisfaction that they have vandalized our lives, but pride never freed anyone. Let yourself actually feel the rage, heartache, and deception. Feel it deeply. Drink it in. Allow yourself to acknowledge that, yes, those particular instances did weaken you, even if it was momentary. The final step can go one of two ways. Sometimes we blow the things that people have done to us out of proportion. We hold on until their actions sting more over time. If this is the case for you, be modest enough to acknowledge it. This is often the way to go for smaller offenses, such as your neighbor's dog or your spouse forgetting your birthday. Another way to finish the forgiveness wheel is to end with the acknowledgment that what this person did was not ok. They don't owe you anything, not an apology, clarification, nothing (Matthew 6:12). The strongest people pardon those who have wronged them, regardless of the type or frequency of the attack (Luke 6:37, Daniel 9:9). However, if you don't feel resilient enough to do so now, take it one day at a time. Jesus told his disciples that if they had faith the size of a mustard seed, they could move mountains (Matthew 13:31). It will be the same for you. All you need is the desire to forgive. Then, work from there.

Activity:

Remember your safety buddy from chapter one? It could be a friend, family member, or trusted loved one. This person has become your confidant, someone you can talk to about your deepest battles. Forgiveness is a difficult gift to present to a person who has so repeatedly wronged you. Vengeance shrieks for justice. Christ calls for forgiveness.

Step one: With your safety buddy, discuss a couple of possible people who you have not forgiven. If you feel like you have no one to forgive, think of it this way. Whenever you see this person, do your muscles tighten up? Do you refuse to ask them for help, no matter how badly you need it? Do you avoid them? Does thinking of what they've done enrage you? Bingo. You've found them. Talk with your safety buddy about the hurt, deception, or abandonment you carry because of this person. Then, discuss the steps you will need to take to begin forgiving them.

Step two: Talk to God about the feelings you have towards this person/these people. Be honest. If you're still angry, even when you don't want to be, let Him know. Our Father in Heaven will not judge.

**Note: if you feel that you are unable to talk about the person who has wronged you, follow this process by journaling it here. (Make sure you're honest with yourself.)

_____
_____
_____
_____
_____
_____
_____
_____
_____
_____
_____
_____
_____
_____
_____
_____

Ending the Competition:

Forgiveness is a complex subject, but there is one specific type t: ending comparisons. I've learned that this form of jealousy is like an atomic bomb- it lays waste to your life for years.

I learned this lesson on a trip home to visit my parents with Nathan.

I wrangled a spindly bike off the back of my dad's white GMC, tires bumping on the rusty trailer hitch as it came down. It was a kid's bike, but better off than the other ones we had. My husband mounted his black cruiser my parents bought off of Facebook marketplace. The August sun was noticeably cooler, so we decided to take a bike ride as we waited for my siblings to return from the Cassia County Fair.

It was immediately evident that my bike was having some serious struggles. The front tire was slightly flat and the gears wobbled my bike forward as I shifted up or down. 500 ft. in I was already panting. By the time we rode half a mile, Nathan pushed several car lengths ahead of me. I stood and pedaled with all my might to catch back up to him, but then quickly fell behind again, sweating more profusely than I thought possible on a relaxing Friday ride.

Frustration welled up in my throat like a shaken soda can. This wasn't the first time this had happened to me. My husband is very athletic and excels at a variety of sports. He played college basketball for two years before meeting me. Every intramural soccer team in Rexburg asked him to be their goalie. He could hit a home run like it was nobody's business, and he had a mean golf game. In the beginning, playing every sport with him caused my heart to sink. I wanted to be good at something, to excel, but I always felt like I was many steps behind my wonderful husband. I stopped seeing my progress and only my flaws. I would count how many times I dropped the baseball or how many baskets I missed compared to my husband. After a while, the frustration developed into a cool determination to beat him at something. I know it sounds silly, but I have always had a competitive bone… a jealous bone.

As we turned around and Nathan sped away from me, I tried to cough away the tears. This was stupid! Why couldn't I just be happy for my husband?

A thought came into my mind, "Did you see the sunflowers?"

I shook it away. How could I look anywhere but right in front of me? I was losing ground by the second. The thought came again, stronger this time. Huffing, I turned my gaze to the side of the road. It was covered in hundreds of sunflowers, their buds reaching up to the sky. My quadriceps slackened in pace as cascading hills of alfalfa stretched before me. Rocky Mountain peaks stretched in every direction as my bike crawled over the dirt road. My husband waited for me at the stop sign, and I studied his face as trucks and tractors ambled by. Long brown eyelashes framed his hazel eyes studded with flecks of green. I thought of the many times he caressed my hair while we chatted about our day. Memories flooded in of the nights we laughed until our sides hurt, and we bounced on the bed because we couldn't sleep. The long car rides. The new adventures. I realized with a start that my envy could easily destroy our relationship. It had done so with so many others. Satan takes whatever he can get and blows it out of proportion. Did I want a life of constant quarrels, bitterness, and eventual hate? Did I want to be the cause of that? I pedaled at my own clip after that, marinating in the realization of my error. My jealousy was linked to selfishness. I wanted to be good. I wished I was more like him. I wished sometimes he wasn't so good. To make myself better, sometimes I wished he wouldn't be so incredible. How ego-centric is that: to wish the downfall of someone else to advance yourself?

I pondered more on the subject. I was so proud of my husband every time he won his various sporting events. Wrapping my arms around his shoulders, we sat in silence after the crushing defeats. But when I put myself into the picture, all I wanted was to win. Immediately. What I came to understand is that my husband put in years of practice and effort to become the athlete he is. Sure, some of that is genetic, but the hours of perfecting every movement in a variety of sports are undeniable. It was time to release my fear of not being good enough.

Resentment can spawn from a feeling of injustice, that you have been wronged somehow. Think about it, why is it fair that Melissa Williams always got the cutest guys in high school just because she was a cheerleader? Why can't you find land a job when your siblings are living their ultra-successful lives?

Mary Baker Edy remarked, "Jealousy is the grave of affection."[10]

And so it is. It's a soul-dividing cancer that spreads and multiplies until your entire being is plagued with it, and as far as mental health goes, it eats away the security of the mind slowly and methodically (Proverbs 6:34-35). Jealous individuals forget Jesus Christ because they're so focused on what everyone else is doing (Doctrine and Covenants 67:10). The more you allow comparison to cloud your judgment the less you see others as people and more as future medals to win. Vindication is short-lived and even shorter-loved. Comparison will follow you to the grave and beyond.

If you have the following thoughts in your mind, it is time to reverse them and rewrite them…

1) I will never be as good as them.

2) They get everything they want (enter your specific example). It's just not fair.

3) I don't get why this happened to them. They're not that special.

4) They don't deserve that. I know their character.

5) Why do good things always happen to them and not me?

This is a tricky topic of forgiveness. We feel in this sense that we have been wronged by others, when really, in this circumstance, we have wronged ourselves. In choosing to repeat that never-ending speech of "why me" and "why them," we add more and more coals to the fire we are walking on. Our feet grow callused and tough, allowing us to pour more into the blaze until we have charred off our ability to walk. In choosing to hold onto our competitive and comparative natures, we are crippling ourselves. We are the ones doing the damage, not them.

My friends, I urge you to be humble and to consider the questions above (Isaiah 57:15). Even if you feel this is not a driving force in your life, we all have something to improve. Let go of your hostility. Forgive yourself for doing so for so long. Choose to let go of the animosity.

If you are unsure of how to do this, ask God! If you ask, you will receive. Know that if you allow this to continue, your life will always be swallowed in breathless heat. Cry out again and again for the Master to heal your blistered life and make way for his matchless love (Psalm 29:11).

IT WON'T ALWAYS BE EASY

Progress is the point of perseverance. If perfection is mostly pending, then our direction is truly more important than speed. My point in writing this book is not to change you. My point is for you to come to the Savior, find healing, and mold yourself into a happier, more fulfilled version of yourself.

But you can't expect it all to come at once, even as you are changing. Run until you feel tired, then walk (Doctrine and Covenants 10:4). Stop if you have to, but don't look back!

I love this quote from a book called *Then Comes Marriage*:

"Our emotional burden will be lifted as we realize that we aren't helpless. This is faith—not the kind of faith that lies passively on a shelf or hidden in a book but the kind that works in the hearts and minds and lives of people. One gift of the gospel is the faith that God is neither a stranger to sorrow nor indifferent to our challenges. As we turn to gospel fundamentals in this way, we will give up the burden of our feelings of helplessness in exchange for faith. Although we will still have feelings, they will be of a different quality altogether than the despair we felt before."[11]

The truth of the matter is that we will all feel helpless at times. There will be days when the Savior will carry us more than we are walking ourselves. Do you ever just feel stuck?

Let Christ carry you in those times. You are getting better every day, though it may be difficult to see. Trust the process. Keep moving forward. You can do this!

Happiness or Joy

Nestled in the farmlands of Idaho, there is a beautiful national reserve called the City of Rocks. Many interesting sights lay there for curious tourists to behold, such as towering boulders, charming trails, an archery range, and a fishing reservoir. My family and I loved visiting, bumping along the potholed backroads that wove in and out of the road. Jackrabbits scurried away as we crunched to a stop in a pea gravel parking lot. My cousins and I plopped bucket hats on our heads and begrudgingly rubbed sunscreen on our arms as we planned our little adventures through the mysterious caves and rocky cliffs. I linked arms with my cousin Mckelle, and we set off hiking, (or maybe more like sprinting). Laughing fearlessly, we scurried to the tops of lofty granite, spooking the rest of our family members as they ambled towards us, herding the toddlers along.

Mckelle and I came to a point in the trail that seemed to veer off in an exciting direction. It was more of a beaten deer path than a man-made one. We exchanged a glance and then sprinted up it. The trees and shrubs grew dense, their branches clawing at our hair as the incline steepened. When we finally emerged from our adventurous side journey, we found ourselves at the top of a steeply declining basalt wall. Only then did we realize how high we had climbed, and fear entered our young hearts. Our family came into view several feet below, and they shouted at us to come down before we hurt ourselves. We had two options: either sidestep the slippery slope to reach the flatter surface several feet above us or try to return down the rocks to our families. We both decided to continue upward. My treaded hiking boots fared better than Mckelle's flat tennis shoes. As she tried to scramble up the rock, her feet slipped, and she skittered down the entire thing. When we came up, her elbows and knees bled profusely, rubbed completely raw from the fall.

As I stood from the top, I found myself questioning, "Was all of that worth it? We worked so hard to climb that mountain just to fall down it again."

Losing our footing can be an unpleasant experience.

The most fascinating part of this experience, however, was not the fall itself; it was the way Mckelle portrayed herself after the fall. Though she sustained nasty scrapes on many parts of her body, she refused to be carried and walked all the way down the mountain, grinning from ear to ear. When people asked where the burns came from, she enjoyed herself greatly by telling them she had fallen off of Bath Rock (the highest climb at the City of Rocks) and survived. Of course, no one believed her, but it drew great laughs from all around. She kept walking, maybe a little more gingerly than before, but she didn't let her fall stop her.

My husband taught me through his ladder analogy that there's a difference between joy and happiness. Joy is something everlasting, that stamps a deep and abiding memory on our souls. Happiness, though also desirable, is momentary, lasting only for a few minutes, maybe an hour. Joy is state of being. Happiness is an emotion which comes and goes.

As you are repenting, evolving, and shaping your life to be like Jesus Christ's, your joy will last for longer and longer. This is you path. This is your destiny. Remember that change is good and never let your fear prevent you from chasing your future.

Sources

1) Nelson, Portia. There's a Hole in My Sidewalk : The Romance of Self-Discovery. New

York, Atria Paperbacks, 2018.

2) Roth, Eric, et al. The Curious Case of Benjamin Button : Screenplay. Calif., Paramount Pictures, 2008.

3) Nelson, President Russell M. "We Can Do Better and Be Better." www.churchofjesuschrist.org, Apr. 2019, www.churchofjesuschrist.org/study/general-conference/2019/04/36nelson?lang=eng.

4) Ulrich, Wendy. Forgiving Ourselves : Getting Back up When We Let Ourselves Down. Salt Lake City, Utah, Deseret Book, 2008.

5) Kearon, Patrick. "God's Intent Is to Bring You Home." Churchofjesuschrist.org, 2024, www.churchofjesuschrist.org/study/general-conference/2024/04/45kearon?lang=eng#p5. Accessed 28 Aug. 2024.

6) Kaouk, Laudy Ruth . "How the Priesthood Blesses Youth." Churchofjesuschrist.org, 2020,www.churchofjesuschrist.org/study/general-conference/2020/04/32alvarez?lang=eng. Accessed 28 Aug. 2024.

7) "Infinite." Merriam-Webster.com Dictionary, Merriam-Webster,

https://www.merriam-webster.com/dictionary/infinite. Accessed 27 Aug. 2024.

8) Lewis, C.S. The Weight of Glory and Other Addresses. London, William Collins, 2013.

9) Montana, Sarah. "Why Forgiveness Is Worth It." Ted.com, TED Talks, 2018,

www.ted.com/talks/sarah_montana_why_forgiveness_is_worth_i t?subtitle=en. Accessed 28 Aug. 2024.

10) Eddy, Mary Baker. "Jealousy Is the Grave of Affection." Goodreads.com, 2020, www.goodreads.com/quotes/137045-jealousy-is-the-grave-of-affection. Accessed 28 Aug. 2024.

11) Ogletree, Mark, and Douglas E Brinley. Then Comes Marriage. American Fork, Utah, Covenant Communications, 2005.

CHAPTER 5: REDEMPTION: GOD'S GRACE

Redeem is not a term that we use educatively (Isaiah 44:22). We use it without understanding what it actually means. A coupon is a worthless piece of paper that when you show up and show it to the store, they will count it as money. A limited understanding portrays the Atonement in this way. Redeem means to buy back, to purchase, to rescue. It's to buy a slave back from the auction and set them free (1 Peter 1:18-19).

We are the ones who always seem to stray from the straight and narrow path. In 1 Nephi 11 the prophet Lehi describes a dream where he was lost in the middle of midnight wilderness. For a while he ambled about aimlessly, crying for someone to aid him. And who did Lehi see first in his vision: a man clothed in white (1 Nephi 8:5-6). It was the Son of the Eternal God leading him to a winding path guided by a rod of iron (1 Nephi 8:19-22). The prophet, his family, and all the people in his vision were instructed to press forward until they reached an exquisite tree. The branches glowed with divine light, mirroring the steadiness of the people who journeyed to reach that destination. Lehi goes on to explain that the fruit of that tree represents the love of God, and it tastes better than any known alimentation (1 Nephi 11:21-23). An interesting twist to this story is that Jesus himself was not at the tree of life. No, He was out in the fog, searching for lost souls. That's the Jesus that I know, and for you to be able to access his reclaiming power, you have to understand that too. The Atonement doesn't only redeem us, it also enables us (Isaiah 40:31)! We will be saved, but we can not remain the way that we are. This is why the Lord asks for continual, gradual improvement, especially with your mind (Doctrine and Covenants 50:40). You don't have to be super depressed in order to take care of your mental health. With the Atonement of Jesus Christ, we don't want to go back to normal, we yearn to push past our earthly limitations! Christ has so much more in store for us (John 17:23-24).

Grace is a word I didn't understand very well a couple of months ago. Why did Christ even choose to redeem us? He lived a perfectly sinless life. Nobody was forcing him to sacrifice himself for us. Yet he did. Like all men before Him, Christ died (Romans 6:10). But no man has ever lived again. When Christ was resurrected, he opened the door for all of us to return to our Father in Heaven (Doctrine and Covenants 63:49). It brings me back to the story of a man in the old country of Norway, many years ago.

The Coal Miner's Son

In the windy mountains of Scandinavia, coal dust choked the air of the peasants who sweated tirelessly to scrape every last bit of coal out of the mountain. It was unlit and glacial, devoid of life beyond the constant chinking of pickaxes against rock, dust tumbling from the chasm into the lungs of mining men. Sometimes mineshafts plummeted down on men, equipment, and hope in one fell swoop (Exodus 15:16).

Such was the life of a coal miner. Dust in the morning, coal in the afternoon, and a warm fire in the evening, with a meager ration of bread and milk. The majority of children barely knew their fathers, and the miner's wives even less.

But there was one miner who was different. When Hans returned to his rock cabin with the last rays of sunlight creeping down the pine trees, he wrapped his arms around his nine children in a bear hug, shouting a battle cry as they engulfed him in a sea of affection. His voice was deep and hearty, like soup with meat and potatoes.

Tossing his youngest daughter into the air, Hans roared with laughter as his sons showed off their wrestling skills. The miner's oldest son, Johan, always followed him through the door a few moments later, equally enthusiastic as nine rowdy children tumbled on top of him. Though this family was undoubtedly the poorest of all the coal scavengers in Scandinavia, every night the father commented on how rich the crusty brown bread tasted on his lips and how he loved his dear wife for making him a king's feast. The children always followed Papa's suit, smacking their lips at the same bread they had also eaten for breakfast. Each night, no matter how late he returned, Hans told all ten of his children a story filled with mischief and wonder. Sometimes when it was very late, a sleepy child begged their papa to stay, to not descend into the filthy pit again. Those children knew better than anyone the cause of a miner's death. They had seen it in their friends and cousin's families again and again. If it was not being crushed in the chasm, it would most assuredly be the black lung when their father was still very young. Often the oldest children woke in the middle of the night, beads of sweat dotting their foreheads as they dreamed of their father being devoured in a merciless tunnel of rock. But Hans never talked of such things. His smile never wavered until one evening in the two room house.

Johan leaned against a window, staring at the moon, only a sliver tonight. He knew his father had something important to say to him. The children slept restlessly near the fire, curling up near each other to try and soak up the warmth. Hans beckoned his oldest son to come closer (1 Nephi 1:1).

"Son." He whispered, "Your mother and I have been thinking for a long time."

Johan's heart beat faster, though he did not know why.

"My grandfather was a coal miner, my father was a coal miner, I am a coal miner, and now you are a coal miner. But you, son, are different from any of those who came before you. You are smart. You are brave. I don't want any more of my children to have to live this life of barely surviving until their papa gets blown out of the sky by a stick of dynamite."

Nodding, Johan acted as if he understood, but he didn't. This was their life, inescapable and endless. What did he have to do with it?

Hans continued, "Your mother and I have saved enough money for you to go to college son. Real college, where you can study, learn, and help your brothers and sisters to leave the mine as well."

Pulling out a crumpled satchel, Hans handed the bag to his son. Johan still did not say a word. Suddenly, Hans' meaty hand shot out and grabbed Johan on the arm, "Son," He said solemnly, "You can save this family. Only you. You were born for this moment; you are our salvation."

So Johan went (Genesis 49:18). The coal miner's son attended the best school in Scandinavia, pouring hours and hours into lifting his knowledge even higher than he thought was possible. In between the classes and study, he worked as a wagon driver, sending home his extra wages to lighten his father's load. Johan loved chemistry with all his heart. Over the years he received his bachelor's degree and became a successful professor in the heart of the mountains. One by one, he brought his siblings with him, pulling them from the frozen wasteland where their father toiled day and night (Matthew 1:20-21). Johan didn't sleep much. The crescent moon reflected off of his father's eyes when Johan grew weary and wished to end his quest. He thought of the black coal cascading down into his brother's eyes or his sisters married to men who constantly lived on the brink of death.

So he worked himself to the bone until every single one of his siblings was safe with him. No more death and despair. No more pits (Job 33:18, 24, 28, 30). No more fear.

Then the news came of Hans' death. Not a regular miner's death of entrapment or asphyxiation; Hans simply went to bed and didn't wake up. After the funeral, Johan's mother tearily handed him a yellowing envelope addressed in a shaky hand.

Johan peeled open the paper and read three words. "We did it."

The day that Jesus Christ spoke to Mary Magdalene outside of his tomb, God said the same thing to his Son, "We did it" (John 20:14-18, Matthew 28:1, Mark 16:9). That's not to say either of them took away our responsibility from our actions (2 Nephi 2:27-29). To be saved doesn't mean that we can do whatever we want and expect to come back to our heavenly home. It's like a mother paying for her son to go to piano lessons. The son goes, but does his practice pay for the piano lessons? No. The price was covered by the child's mother. The way for him to repay her was to follow her conditions: practice.

Because Jesus rose from the dead, that is a free gift for all mankind (2 Nephi 2:4). We will have life again someday (Moses 7:62, Job 14:14). But our actions in this life will determine where we end up when that time comes.

Johan brought all of his siblings to a safer plane, but could he control every one of their actions after that? No, nor would he want to. That wasn't his father's intention either. They simply wished to spare them the fate of inevitable darkness and death (Hosea 13:14). That is exactly what our Heavenly Father saved us from as well, by allowing his firstborn son to die for us.

149

That's grace. That's redemption. It's doing our best for our Lord, using repentance, and recognising that every day, we can try again. But we must try.

You are trying to do something that may seem impossible to you right now. You're taming Big Meanie and fear, all the while developing into the person God wants you to be. It's a bit daunting, isn't it?

Then people fall onto the flipside of grace, where they may say, "I've made too many mistakes. I can't recover from this."

To illustrate the Savior's kindness, I share the account of another father and his sons.

Grace

A religion teacher at BYU-Idaho shared this timeless story on the principle of grace. My professor was close with his brother in law, who we will call Jeff. Every couple years, Jeff indulged in buying a new truck. He traded out the current, shiny model he possessed and bartered it for another of higher value. As was his tradition, Jeff always hunted for the best deals, scouting different dealerships and locations to pinpoint which vehicle would be the most ideal for him and his family. Jeff was also the proud father of two rambunctious boys named Sam and Jake. These children often kept their mother busy, so one sunny Saturday, Jeff told their mother he would watch the hooligans. It was beautiful weather in Arizona, the sun just beginning to show her classic summer heat, so Jeff herded his sons outside to play in the yard before it became too hot for their little bodies. Though he watched them play for a while, Jeff's phone buzzed with an incoming call. He picked up and left the kids to continue their antics in the yard. Jake and Sam decided to play in the water because the weather was deliciously warm. Jake, the older of the two, pointed at Daddy's truck.

"It's pretty dirty!" He exclaimed, "We should help Daddy clean it!"

Sammy threw his hands up in the air, "But we have no wags (rags) to wash it with."

Jake pondered that statement. This was true. His six-year-old mind spun until a fateful idea struck him, "I know!" He said, "We will wash it with rocks!"

Scott, finishing his phone call, returned to the backyard. The boys were not there. Coasting to the front door, he discovered the tragic news. His two children flashed him toothy grins. "Look daddy! Your truck is all clean now!"

It was not clean. Circular grooves lined the front and sides of the vehicle, deeply contrasting the sparkling red paint that remained "unwashed." For a moment, anger welled up in Scott's chest. His brand new truck was completely destroyed by swirling scratches deeply etched into the doors and hood. What would justice have done in this situation (Zechariah 7:9)? Spankens obviously! Punishment! But what did this father do? He went into the house and pulled otter pops out of the freezer, sat them down on the porch, and told them how much he loved them (Proverbs 22:6). Then, and only then, did he explain the error of their ways. This is grace. Grace flows from Christ's bounteous mercy (1 Chronicles 16:34). It's everlasting. It never ends. That's what redemption is. It's getting what you don't deserve, despite all that you've done.

Some have asked me why I chose to include repentance and redemption in a book about mental health. And I pose the same question: why not? Why not remind you that you are capable of change and worthy of love? This is your time to believe it!

We should all plead for mercy on judgment day . I hope no one says on judgment day, "I just want what I deserve." God gives what is undeserved to us. Jesus not only forgives us of our sins, he awards us with what we could never earn (Matthew 25:34). If you haven't realized how good the gospel is, this is a testament of it. What saves you, a prescription or taking the medicine? It's the medicine that saves you, not taking it. Though there are many good things in the world, only Jesus Christ can rescue us. All of the vertical movement in the gospel is Jesus' responsibility. You do the horizontal movement. You come to Christ and He brings you to God. No matter how good you are in this life, Jesus Christ is the reason you can return to your Heavenly Father.

That's why salvation is a gift, and it can't be earned. The only thing we can do is put ourselves in a position to achieve it by continually striving to become better (not perfect).

When we are at our low points, Satan will come at us with everything he has. He did the same when Christ fasted for forty days and forty nights in the wilderness (Matthew 4:1-11). When the pressure mounts upon your head for you to retreat, know that God knows your every need, sometimes even before you ask for his help (Matthew 6:8). To illustrate this point, I'd like to share the story of my sheep, Piper.

Injured

Rabbitbrush and pinon pines by as my dad and I jostled over the grubby Arco road. We were hunting for antelope, or at least my dad was. This time I was selected to be the designated antelope spotter. Unfortunately, I wasn't very good at my job. A juicy hamburger with a sizzling tray of fries played on repeat in my mind, bringing a bucket full of saliva into my mouth. My stomach grumbled unhappily.

Then, my hand-me-down phone vibrated under my leg. It was my mom. She called explaining that one of my sheep had been attacked by a neighbor's dog, and now her leg was mangled beyond repair.

Let me back up here. I've mentioned before that the majority of my life was spent on hundreds of acres of farmland teeming with a variety of animals: dogs, cows, chickens, ducks, llamas, horses, donkeys, and, my personal favorite, sheep. I love sheep (Psalm 78:52). Because of their natural fight-or-flight instincts, sheep are very wary creatures, so I spent hours at a time lying out in the straw, patiently waiting for the ewes and lambs to approach me. I sheared off mountains of wool from their backs so the scalding summer sun wouldn't fry them alive. In the wintertime, my mom and I plodded in the crunchy snow to the cherry-colored barn at three in the morning to help the mama sheep give birth to her young.

By the time I was fourteen, my mom allowed me to buy a couple of my own sheep to breed and sell (Psalm 95:7). I knew all of them by name and their distinctive bleats (John 10:27, Psalm 147:1,3-5). The skinny black lambs kicked up their legs and frolicked around me when I hauled a heavy water bucket over the fence. My best breeding ewe was named Piper. Because of her defiant nature, the other sheep recognised her as the leader of the herd.

My mouth gaped open at the videos my mom sent me. I imagined the music from Jaws playing as the camera wheeled on Piper's lacerated leg. I nearly gagged. Raw flesh hung in shreds from the ewe's back end, leaving a ghastly hole where sinew and skin should have been. When we returned home from hunting I immediately hurried out to the feed shack where my grandpa and my mom shook their heads at the hideous sight. Piper baa-ed forlornly, her eyes cloudy from the extreme pain. My grandpa advised us to put the poor sheep out of her misery, but I leaped in between them.

"No!" I yelled, "Just let me try to fix her leg. She's my favorite sheep, and she's tough."

Grandpa hedged at my abrupt outburst, "Emree," He soothed, "It's just a sheep. Look at her. She's miserable."

I understood my lamb more than anyone else could. I couldn't let Piper die without attempting to recover her. Eventually, I convinced my mother and grandfather that if I took care of Piper's leg, I could endeavor to save her, as long as she wasn't in too much pain (1 Nephi 22:25).

The first couple of days were rough. It was a warm fall that year, which meant the flies and bugs buzzed in full force. Even though we sprayed the gaping hole with wound spray and covered it with my dad's grubby t-shirts, after a week Piper's leg oozed with puss and maggots. Again, my grandpa shook his head and recommended we put the sheep down. Again, I threw my arms around the dejected ewe and said, "Give her a little more time" (Jacob 5:26-27).

Weeks passed. I administered many shots with life-saving medicine and rubbed the gaping laceration with alcohol to kill the maggots (3 Nephi 15:24). Piper improved daily. My grandpa stopped proposing that we let the sheep pass. Everyone watched with amazement the recovery of a seemingly hopeless situation (Ether 12:8).

Three years later, Piper was still on the farm. Miraculously, the muscle and fat that had been clawed out by a vicious dog's jaws grew back, though maybe not as strong as before. I smiled proudly at my precious sheep. Though she hobbled with a slight limp, her mind was as fierce as the day I saved her life.

I think about her from time to time: my warrior sheep. You know, she probably didn't feel like too much of a trooper the day she was attacked and left for dead, but I wasn't going to leave her like that. I knew her worth, and I wasn't about to let her die on me.

Jesus Christ is our good Samaritan, He is a good shepherd, and He is the lamb (Luke 10:30-34, John 10:11, 1 Nephi 12:11). You may ask yourself how this is possible, for someone to be both the physician and the patient. This is the Atonement of Jesus Christ stripped down to its barest bones (2 Nephi 9:7). Before his suffering in Gethsemane, Christ had perfect empathy (Matthew 9:36). His perfection allowed him to perceive people's thoughts and cure them of chronic diseases. But it was through his anguish in Gethsemane that Christ experienced what we felt. In his flawlessness, he chose to undergo our imperfection (Mosiah 15:9). He healed our imperfections in advance, but he didn't take away our ability to decide for ourselves. That's why your mental health matters to Christ. That's why when you can't begin to describe your tortured soul to another person on the planet, Christ knows, and He empowers you to overcome it. How? First, He binds up our wounds (Psalm 147:3). Then He delivers us to a place where we feel safe (Proverbs 29:25). Once we are on the mend, He remains near us, He pays the price again and again for our injuries. Just like Piper, the Savior will not leave us to die. Your life can be restored through Him.

President Nelson shared these touching remarks regarding the subject, "Please know this: if everything and everyone else in the world whom you trust should fail, Jesus Christ and His Church will never fail you. The Lord never slumbers, nor does He sleep. He "is the same yesterday, today, and [tomorrow]." He will not forsake

His covenants, His promises, or His love for His people. He works miracles today, and He will work miracles tomorrow. Faith in Jesus Christ is the greatest power available to us in this life. All things are possible to them that believe.

Your growing faith in Him will move mountains—not the mountains of rock that beautify the earth but the mountains of misery in your lives. Your flourishing faith will help you turn challenges into unparalleled growth and opportunity."[1]

I've pondered many different scenarios which transpire on our journey to understand ourselves and our Master more. Sometimes these thoughts flow naturally. We often forget to reach out to Christ, even though we know He can and will deliver us. We may believe that Christ is our strength and our salvation, but the application of stretching ourselves for his aide is slightly more complicated than we care to admit (Exodus 15:2). Why? We're human. We overload our lives with meaningless things and tumble into a radical state of general unhappiness before we recall the Son of the Living God (2 Nephi 31:16). Such was my state of mind when I clattered away on my computer on the final day of summer.

Write My Words

I was stuck: completely mired in what I should put together for this chapter. My first summer as a married woman was coming to an end, and I caught a case of severe writer's block. I bargained and complained to God in alternating intervals like a teenager begging their parents for a new phone (Exodus 16:1-15).

"Please God!" I harrumphed, "I'm doing this for other people!"

Other times...

"Ok, Heavenly Father," I started tentatively, "Am I being wicked in some way? Am I breaking some law I didn't know about?"

This carried on for almost a week. Occasionally an inkling of an idea floated into my skull, so I scooped it up and tapped it down on my laptop (most of this chapter is a result of that) (Isaiah 28:9-10). I begged God for the ability to write for hours on end, to have loads of story designs that would wow my readers. Instead, I felt random promptings to chat with a friend who I hadn't talked to in a while. I played a board game with my sister. I devoted quality time to my husband. After each instance, my heart caught the wind like a bird in flight. It was as if I released spring-loaded tension from my skeleton. Instead of pouring hours into staring at my computer, I took care of myself and the people around me. The scriptures came to life about the people I was helping, and in a way, those people were helping me too (Matthew 25:40).

We learned in Chapter Two about those nasty "duty words," you know, the things you think you should be doing, but don't really have the heart to accomplish. Let me break this down for you. Your body's framework runs on glucose, including your brain.[2] Imagine an ultramarathoner who decides to undergo a 100 mile race in the desert with no food, water, or bathroom breaks. It sounds impossible, doesn't it? That's how your mind operates as well. It can only go for so long, even with extensive training, and it can only do so many things in one day. There are millions of tasks we may undergo in the course of the day, but we may only finish a few. This is because of the unbudging pace of time. When we jam too many options of what we want into a shortened time to complete them, we shove God out of the picture. So, occasionally God takes things into his own hands.

This was the case with me when I forced myself to complete something that was really God's work. Words didn't flow, Ideas evaded me like sleep on Christmas, and I was infuriated. I wanted my goal completed in my time and my way, but that's not how God's timing works.

No, I grumbled and groaned for many days before I decided to sit back and question what God wanted me to compose. His response came to me one day when I least expected it. After a week of seemingly little inspiration, the thought occurred to me, "Write my words."

My brain nearly exploded. I resisted the urge to whine, "I'm trying!"

Suddenly, a short film replayed in my mind of the past week. I had written, however slowly, and now had a substantial chapter. Was it perfect? No. Was it done in the time that I wanted? Also no.

Again, the voice repeated softly, "Write my words."

This time, I bowed my head and repeated, "I will write your words God. Please forgive me for doing this on my own."

It was then this chapter began God's way (Alma 7:23-25).

I want you to ponder that for a moment. God's way. What does that mean for you? Are you resisting him?

Activity: God's Way

Simple ways to determine if you might be resisting God's way:[3]

1) Your mind is all over the place, and you feel a certain numbness.

2) You're too tired to do things that used to be fun for you.

3) You get irritated easily with other people.

4) You are trying to do the "right things," but you still feel empty.

5) You struggle to exercise or even move sometimes.

I find number four the most frustrating of all of these symptoms. Sometimes I am reading my scriptures, saying my prayers, giving to the homeless, going to church, and am on the verge of donating my right kidney, because it is the "right thing" (Moroni 8:2). This is where the "shoulds" and "have-to's" growl menacingly. Just because you are doing many good things doesn't mean that you are completing what God wishes for you to accomplish. You're following your plan, not His. Mental exhaustion originates from an overworked mind (Mosiah 4:27). Like the marathoner, if you try to go too long without doing the things God intends for you, you will lose steam.

Those things aren't always what you would expect either. Sometimes you are giving too much of yourself to other people. If you completely empty your metaphorical pitcher of lemonade to everyone else around you, then you will have none for yourself. It's a balance that comes from listening.

Every instance will be different. That's the importance of learning to hear divine guidance.

Listening:

Take a deep breath.

Conduct a self inquiry on how you feel at the end of the day. Exhausted? Run down? (If you feel great, wait to continue until you do reach an evening where these feelings come.)

What are some possible causes of this depletion? Are you balancing too many things on your plate? Are you allowing yourself time to relax? Have you looked at the needs of other people?

Finally, ask God what He wants you to do.

Repeat for as long as necessary. Prepare yourself to do some serious humbling. I suggest not griping as I did, but truly asking Heavenly Father with a penitent heart what you should do.

***Note: Sometimes if you don't secure a response, understand that this may be God trusting you to make the decision for yourself. Do you see where the balance plays in here?

Brittany

A paintbrush picks up dabs of thick acrylic paint in its bristles, smoothly draping a sky over a white house. The artist plunges her tool into another shade of ebony, draping a chipped sidewalk next to a drooping picket fence. A teenager with thundercloud eyes and fluffy pigtails is depicted on the porch, one hand on her cheek as she wonders what else might be out there. Paint smears onto the canvas in an intricate dance, slipping and sliding into a memory. There's one peculiarity to this work of art: it's all monochrome. Thousands of tones of gray with hues of a kaleidoscope, but never leaving the cool silver glint. The creator stands back and sighs, rubbing her thumb against the dried paint on her hands. All of her paintings are in black and white, because that's all she's ever known.

Our creator comprehends affliction. He comprehends backstories and future stories. Sometimes we lose sight of what matters most, but Christ doesn't. I gained this wisdom from my friend, Brittany. Here are her words:

"I struggle with anxiety, PTSD, depression, and ADHD. That's the base of what I'mm about to say.

I grew up with my mom for the majority of my life. I love her a lot, but there are a lot of negative things that stemmed from how I was raised. My mom was very emotionally and verbally abusive. There was a lot of emotional neglect. As a result, I wasn't aggressive, but I concealed how I felt. It's taken me a long time to learn how to communicate with people because I was afraid of how they would respond. Partially I also did it to shield my mom, but true love is being vulnerable enough to share that you're hurting, and it's their fault.

Despite this trauma, my mom was always my superstar. Because my biological father was very abusive, I always clung to her. I gravitated towards stability. Eventually we left that situation with my father, and my mom shouldered the burden of caring for all of her children. Because of the horrors she experienced, my mom eased into more verbal aggression as the years went on. I had no one to turn to.. I mastered being tough. My mom taught me to bury emotions until we decomposed into a state of numbness. But even through all of these struggles, I maintained a strong connection to God. Even when my mom projected her inner conflict on me, I still relied on God and my Savior.

When I was fifteen I came across two men in white shirts and ties. We lived in a rough neighborhood in Florida, and it was pretty late to be roaming out and about.; I was draped on the porch drawing in my notebook when I spotted two guys in white shirts talking about "hitting the last house." As the rounded the corner, I nearly dashed for the door, but to my surprise, I felt something tell me to stay. By the time they arrived at our battered steps, I radiated complete peace (1 Corinthians 14:33). The two of them asked me about God. I replied that I was a Baptist. Then they questioned what I understood about Jesus. My chest swelled with warmth, like how you feel when you learn a concept in class and it rings true to you. I stared at their shiny black name tags and thought, "This is different. This is special." Even so, I was scared. I shared everything I could about Jesus Christ and went into as much depth as I could.

This is me, a young child in the ghetto. My mom left me to sit with two young men. She didn't want anything to do with them.

When they told me I was a daughter of God, it rocked my world (Deuteronomy 14:1). I'd never felt valued in my life. When I heard the things that Jesus said to his disciples, relief finally surfaced (Matthew 5). After all of those years wondering if I would ever be able to fix my family, my fears washed away in my thankful tears. Sure, I had my bad habits, but they couldn't hold me down anymore. I felt like a new person (Ezekiel 11:19). That peace I later found was the Holy Ghost (3 Nephi 11:3). The more I came to know Jesus, the more that spirit remained with me, like a friend when it all seemed like too much. Through Jesus Christ, I found my worth.

We kept meeting, and I kept feeling the spirit so strong. God was so aware of me. This whole time, I was very depressed. My mom was angry with me. My parents were very abusive with each other. That's hard to face as a child. I found more self-worth in my identity as a child of God.

Through the lens that I had, I painted everything in my world as black and white. I was color blind to the possibilities available to me. When the missionaries came, it was like a vibrant color, like a living fire within me. When I was with my family, those colors faded away. Eventually, I saw the world as it really was. Christ brought that color back into my life.

An important thing to note is that I didn't know what a testimony of Jesus Christ was before (2 Timothy 1:8). I knew of

Christ.. I appreciated that He died on the cross. That was enough for me at the time, but I didn't have a relationship with Him- not even close. As I explored the scriptures, intensified my prayers, and and enhanced my relationship with Jesus Christ, the depression inched away from me little by little (1 Nephi 2:10).,Christ was on my side. When I see things from Christ's perspective, it drags me out of my spiraling thoughts. Spiraling for me equals increased depression. The spirit is almost nonexistent when I am in the thick of it. In these moments, I ground myself to what I know is stable (Helaman 5:12). I've learned to rely on both my husband and the Savior (Genesis 2:18). For example, when I'm under a wave of apathy because I didn't talk about something I should have, my husband Ezra can tell when I'm off. Talking is so important to me. Another source of stability for me is the Book of Mormon and the Bible.

I still love my mom. From her I learned to be resilient and to stay strong in uncertain circumstances. .

When I began to fortify my relationship with Jesus Christ, I often lingered in between the darkness and the vibrant color. I always attended church on my own. The people in my ward recognised my struggle with returning to my mom. I felt horrible when I was with her. At the same time, I felt responsible to take care of her. That's how we had survived in the past, looking out for each other, even if the method wasn't the most effective. Eventually I made the decision to move away from my mom. I always clung to her because I believed I had no choice. When I visited some of my friend's homes, tranquility returned. The difference was tangible. I was in a safe place: a no judgment zone. When I returned home, my mom crashed over me, cussing at me, and making me feel worthless again. I thought I didn't need to feel that way anymore.

Jesus Christ mends all wounds. All of them. Sometimes to see those rich colors, you have to let go. I resisted the Savior's call for so long because I was terrified of what I would lose (Acts 7:51). It took a lot of trust to trade my dark paint bottles out for Christ's vivid colors (John 1:4-9). I didn't understand the tones at first, but, gradually, I replaced my perception for Christ's broader perspective. My entire life shimmered. Now when I paint, my art reflects my life (Matthew 16:25). The art is no longer a frightened girl in charcoal and ivory, but a woman hand in hand with her husband, striding towards the Savior (Mosiah 2:6).

I've pondered many different scenarios that occur to us on our journey to understand ourselves and our Master more. Sometimes these thoughts flow naturally. But more often than not we forget to reach out to Christ, even though we know He can and will deliver us (Joel 2:32). We may believe that Christ is our strength and our salvation, but the application of reaching for his aide is slightly more complicated than we care to admit (Exodus 15:2). Why? We're human. We overload our lives with meaningless things and tumble into a radical state of general unhappiness before we recall the Son of the Living God (2 Nephi 31:16). Such was my state of mind when I clattered away on my computer on the final day of summer.

Write My Words

I was stuck: completely mired in what I should put together for this chapter. My first summer as a married woman was coming to an end, and I caught a case of severe writer's block. I bargained and complained to God in alternating intervals like a teenager begging their parents for a new phone (Exodus 16:1-15).

"Please God!" I harrumphed, "I'm doing this for other people!"

Other times…

"Ok, Heavenly Father," I started tentatively, "Am I being wicked in some way? Am I breaking some law I didn't know about?"

This carried on for almost a week. Occasionally an inkling of an idea floated into my skull, so I scooped it up and tapped it down on my laptop (most of this chapter is a result of that) (Isaiah 28:10). I begged God for the ability to write for hours on end, to have loads of story designs that would wow my readers. Instead, I felt random promptings to chat with a friend who I hadn't talked to in a while. I played a board game with my sister. I devoted quality time to my husband. After each instance, my heart caught the wind like a bird in flight (1 Nephi 1:15). It was as if I released spring-loaded tension from my skeleton. Instead of pouring hours into staring at my computer, I took care of myself and the people around me (John 13:34-35). The scriptures came to life about the people I was helping, and in a way, those people were helping me too (Matthew 25:40).

We learned in Chapter Two about those nasty "duty words," you know, the things you think you should be doing, but don't really have the heart to accomplish. Let me break this down for you. Your body's framework runs on glucose, including your brain. Imagine an ultramarathoner who decides to undergo a 100 mile race in the desert with no food, water, or bathroom breaks. It sounds impossible, doesn't it?

That's what I swam through when I tried to force myself to complete something that was really God's work. I wanted it in my time and my way, but that's not how God's timing works.

No, I grumbled and groaned for many days before I decided to sit back and question what God wanted me to compose. His response came to me one day when I least expected it. After a week of seemingly little inspiration, the thought occurred to me, "Write my words."

My brain nearly exploded. I resisted the urge to whine, "I'm trying!"

Suddenly, a short film replayed in my mind of the past week. I had written, however slowly, and now had a substantial chapter. Was it perfect? No. Was it done in the time that I wanted? Also no. Despite all of this, I knew I created this chapter God's way. And if I spent more time observing and less time whining, I would have seen it sooner.

I want you to ponder that for a moment. God's way (John 14:6).

What does that mean for you? Are you resisting him?

Activity: God's Way

Simple ways to determine if you might be resisting God's way:[3]

1) Your mind is all over the place, and you feel a certain numbness.

2) You're too tired to do things that used to be fun for you.

3) You get irritated easily with other people.

4) You're trying to do the "right things," but you still feel empty.

5) You struggle to exercise or even move sometimes.

I find number four the most frustrating of all of these symptoms. Sometimes I am reading my scriptures, saying my prayers, giving to the homeless, going to church, and am on the verge of donating my right kidney, because it is the "right thing." This is where the "shoulds" and "have-to's" growl menacingly.

Just because you are doing many good things doesn't mean that you are completing what God wishes for you to accomplish . You're following your plan, not His. Mental exhaustion originates from an overworked mind (Mosiah 4:27). Like the marathoner, if you try to go too long without doing the things God intends for you, you will lose steam.

Those things aren't always what you would expect either. Sometimes you are giving too much of yourself to other people. If you completely empty your metaphorical pitcher of lemonade to everyone else around you, then you will have none for yourself. It's a balance that comes from listening.

Every instance will be different. That's the importance of learning to hear divine guidance.

Listening:

Take a deep breath.

Conduct a self inquiry on how you feel at the end of the day. Exhausted? Run down? (If you feel great, wait to continue this part until you do reach an evening where these feelings come.)

What are some possible causes of this depletion? Are you balancing too many things on your plate? Are you allowing yourself time to relax? Have you looked at the needs of other people?

Finally, ask God what He wants you to do.

Repeat for as long as necessary. Prepare yourself to do some serious humbling. I suggest not griping as I did, but truly asking Heavenly Father with a penitent heart what you should do.

***Note: Sometimes if you don't secure a response, understand that this may be God trusting you to make the decision for yourself. Do you see where the balance plays in here?

Jesus

Fulfilling the will of God is easier when we remember what He did.

All his life, our Savior gave. As I considered the amount of people he daily taught and administered to, I realized how relieved He must have been when He finally gasped out the words, "It is finished" (John 19:30)

Christ's cross was heavy. Not only had He been beaten severely and starved, He dragged a 150 lb cross across the city to the hill where He would soon hang until His time came (John 19:17, Matthew 27:28-31). Splinters split into Jesus' raw flesh as his shoulders trembled from exertion, one determined step after the other. Though the searing lash marks on that sinless back stung and blood seeped into Christ's eyes from His taunting crown, He didn't buckle under that beam's crushing weight. One step, then another. Shaking, pulverizing, steps. How could He bear it? Across the crowd there were some who had followed him. There were more who jeered and taunted, calling him the "King of the Jews" (Matthew 27:37). Yet, He endured it. Why did He continue? Because the Messiah's cross was not nearly as heavy as the trillions He had carried the night before. In the dusky twilight of the twisting trees whispering in the gentle Mount of Olives, he bore YOUR fear. The day you felt like an absolute loser? He bore it. The day you asked yourself what all of this was for? He bore it. The day you endured another round of personal assault, catapulting yourself to the edge, he bore it. His grace is sufficient.

You can't repay the Lord for what He did for you. You can't work yourself to the bone and look at the neverending list of things you didn't accomplish and exclaim, "How can I ever repay this debt?"

In Doctrine and Covenants section 45, it says, "Wherefore, Father, spare these my brethren that believe on my name, that they may come unto me and have everlasting life."

Though Jesus did it for us, He also did it for Himself. He had all the agency in the world to turn back. Christ could have shied away from His responsibility, but we all came to earth to be tested, and we all arrived with a mission. Christ's test was even greater than ours because He manifested the greatest loyalty to the Father.

In his infinite act of will, Christ demonstrated the grit and determination it takes to stay with God no matter the cost. We can hold on. We will make it. We can do all things with Christ (Moroni 10:23).

When Jesus Christ approaches God's judgment seat, He won't say anything about you. There's no mention of the time you called Aunt Bea fat behind her back or when you shattered one of your mom's plates and lied about it. He doesn't mention the people you hurt, the times you screamed that you didn't want God's help, or that you didn't even believe in His existence. Nor does the Lamb of God present your positive qualities. He doesn't say, well, cut her some slack, she's a good person, just let her go. Jesus is the advocate and the defendant. He doesn't accuse you, and He doesn't label you. With those brilliant blue eyes, He opens his scarred palms and says to the jury, "Don't look at them. Look at me. Their crimes are irrelevant because I took them. I slapped them upon my back so that they wouldn't have to brave their voyage alone. Their sins do not belong to them. They belong to me. So, judge me."

Jesus says spare us, because He is perfect. The jury has absolutely nothing against Jesus Christ because He was flawless. There is not one attorney in the world that can defend his client based on his own merits. A lawyer can not shield a person convicted of first degree murder by saying that he himself has never done wrong. Christ can do that. Because He is good, we are saved. God wants to forgive our sins. The angels look at our testimonies and weep, because they know that Christ holds us in His perfect hands.

Do you realize what that means for you? When you acknowledge your faults to God, keep His commandments, and strive to improve, you will be guaranteed a place with Him in his mansions above (John 14:2). Your mental health can lift you! With Christ, your weaknesses will be transformed into redeeming resilience. You can do this.

Activity: Dare to Dream

Sometimes when we hyperfocus on a goal- our imperfections or possible scenarios that could occur- we lose focus of our infinite capacity. Our destiny blurs out of focus, and in the midst of the chaos, we forget to dream (Roman 8:24, Joel 3:16). It takes guts to believe that tomorrow will be better. Because of Jesus Christ, our lives will be better.

Your life is incredible, but screaming inner thoughts can tear us away from the things we love most. I find this happens quite often with adults. Because we don't believe in Christmas or the Easter Bunny anymore, we lose our zest for life. Old hobbies and things that enveloped us in satisfaction fade to oblivion. We choose to scroll our lives away when any scrap of attention presents itself to us. Where is your dream? What were things you always wished to do as a younger version of you? Did you long to paint masterpieces to sell through your own online business? Did you picture yourself backpacking through Europe? Owning a hobby farm? Bungee jumping? Seeing your favorite professional sports team?

I see far too often that when people understand the Atonement, they believe that they must deny themselves of their dreams. Do you realize that Jesus Christ is the one who allows you to hope? Without Him, there would be nothing.

Think hard. Write down a couple of things that you used to enjoy or dream of doing. Why did you stop? Were you too busy? Or did you believe it would never come true? Ponder to yourself, "How can I make this dream happen with Jesus Christ?" Finally pray for his assistance (that's the magic ingredient).

Dream_____

Dream_____

Dream_____

How can I make this Dream Happen with Jesus Christ?

Trusting in redemption:

I didn't always depend on Christ's gift as much as I do now because I didn't believe I was good enough for him. It took time for me to learn to dream again, and one of the pivotal things that moved me forward was my friend Kylie. Kylie often studied with me after our microbiology class at BYU Idaho. She is an absolute gem. Sweet doesn't even begin to describe her; that girl is absolutely the kindest, most thoughtful person I've ever met. Generally after we finished class, we scoured the Benson building for an empty room to rewrite information on the stained whiteboards. We indulged in small side conversations as we worked, gradually shaping our friendship. Kylie's black curly hair, pulled expertly back into a cute ponytail, bobbed up and down as she bounced between her notes to the whiteboard where she was drawing. I sketched out a process with a red dry-erase marker. The room smelled of formaldehyde and dusty old microscopes. The weekend before had been difficult for me. I still grappled with feeling insufficient for God, and my emotions bled into my work like overturned Coca-Cola on an eighth-grade English paper (John 6:5, 7-9). As I scratched a scraggly portrait of a B-cell, the distinct impression came to my mind to ask Kylie what she did when she felt overwhelmed. I overturned it immediately, rationalizing that my friend didn't want to converse with me about that, nor did we have time to waste with finals week coming up. The impression entered again, so strongly this time that the words flew out of my mouth in a torrent.

Kylie quirked her beautiful black eyebrow at me. I had never asked her a question so personal before. I almost retracted the statement when, to my surprise, she began to cry. Kylie, like I, felt alone. Though she fasted and prayed and worked to do everything within her power to find her future spouse, still, at age 29, she remained painfully single. Her heart wrenched every time she witnessed another happy couple holding hands or pushing a pink-faced baby on the snowy Rexburg sidewalk. Every prayer, Kylie pleaded with Heavenly Father to send someone to give her companionship.

"What am I doing wrong?" My friend cried out to God in anguish, "What more can I do?"

She doubted herself because that's what everyone else did for her. Kylie carried many blows from people she once thought she could trust. Slicing, biting words from Kylie's past carved a hole in her present, and there she remained, the girl with holes. Contempt oozed from their hateful statements, and Kylie wondered if it were better to believe them. She was broken (Psalm 69:20). Too broken? That, my dear companion, didn't know.

We cried together across the table in that musty lab room, and I admitted how weak I felt recently, how I didn't know if I could ever be good enough for God. Though I knew they were lies, often I assumed that God wouldn't love me if I didn't do everything in my power to please him so I could be right with him on judgment day. We were two women, women with holes. Kylie's holes began with the shovels of others; mine I excavated for myself. Regardless, our hearts hung, fractured, and limp within our chests.

Kylie gave an interesting analogy that sticks with me to this day. After a few minutes to gain our composure, I asked Kylie how she did it, what kept her going when the depression was so heavy, the burden so unbearable (Matthew 23:4). One solitary tear slipped onto her freckled cheeks, yet this one radiated so distinctly from the others. This was her story of strength (2 Samuel 22:33).

"There are many times," Kylie admitted, "That I feel like the woman at the well (John 4:6-15). I walk many miles to draw water and return with it to my apartment. This water is what keeps me going on the days that the sun beats down on me, and my feet throb from wandering in the scalding desert sand. Recently, when I finally arrived at my well and collapsed near its mouth, I discovered the contents had dried up. My well of relief is empty. My dry lips tremble, and salty sweat burns my eyes nearly as much as the tears. Those are my darkest moments when I question if I will die of thirst (Psalm 42:1-3). But I always dip my bucket in any way. I lower it down slowly and hear the dusty clank as it hits a meaningless bottom. Then I draw it up again. The bucket grows heavier. It takes more of my exertion to drag the cord to the top. To my astonishment, when I heave my bucket close to my face, it's completely full. I can't believe my eyes. I peer into the well again. Empty. As I drink the water, it's the cleanest and purest my tongue has ever tasted. I drink until I can drink no more. I'm filled (Isaiah 55:1)."

She stared at me, ebony eyes bright with untold courage, "I don't know how I'm going to make it another day sometimes. There are days I don't even want to be here," Kylie's soft voice cracked, "But I know that Jesus Christ fills my bucket every single day, even when I feel that I have no more to give, even when I am not sure how to continue or where to go. I know Jesus Christ lives, and for now, that is enough for me."

1 Peter 1:6 reads, "Because it is written, Be ye holy; for I am holy."

Both Kylie and I considered ourselves to be women with holes. Perhaps you've seen yourself that way as well: a portion of a person with pieces taken from your soul. Well, I have news for you. Try changing the wording of this sentence. A person with holes could also be described as a *holey person.* Holey means to allow passage in and out. The word Holy (without the e) means sacred, consecrated, or hallowed. Why is it that God asks us, as his covenant children, to wear the sacred garment when we are of the proper age? It's a symbol of Christ's Atonement. Though Adam and Eve fell, though they made the unthinkable mistake, the only mistake available to them, God gave them the coat of skin (Genesis 3:21). God reminded them that if they would only make a covenant with him, He would give them someone to take care of them, someone to take away the pain. Our Savior saves us from ourselves. He fills our *holes* and makes us *whole (Matthew 9:21).* Though we and others have used our spades to dig out the good from ourselves, Christ is right behind us, ready to fill in the chasms with his own two hands. Kylie needed God's grace. She needed his mercy. Though her prayer has not been contested in the the way that she expected for herself, her salvation is already free (2 Nephi 2:4). Let Christ change you from one *holey* to the other, the higher and nobler form.

Stay

Now for the final piece of the puzzle. We've pursued topics of identity, Christ's love, and our potential to succeed. For many, when life batters them down and tears at their flickering resolve, it seems easier to step away from Jesus. The world trend is falling away from Christianity. How can we be so foolish to believe in someone we can't see? This is where our faith becomes an anchor against the roiling tides. When you feel tempted to retreat because you think you don't have what it takes, consider this last section.

Elder D. Todd Christofferson said, "Because of the infinite virtue of His great atoning sacrifice, Jesus Christ can satisfy or 'answer the ends of the law' on our behalf. Pardon comes by the grace of Him who has satisfied the demands of justice by His own suffering, 'the just for the unjust, that He might bring us to God' (1 Peter 3:18). He removes our condemnation without removing the law. We are pardoned and placed in a condition of righteousness with Him. We become, like Him, without sin. We are sustained and protected by the law, by justice. We are, in a word, justified. Thus, we may appropriately speak of one who is justified as pardoned, without sin, or guiltless…To be sanctified through the blood of Christ is to become clean, pure, and holy. If justification removes the punishment for past sin, then sanctification removes the stain or effects of sin."[4]

It always ruins someone's day when they find out that cucumbers are pickles. If it ruins yours, there's counseling available to you. The process of concocting a bubbling brine with spices, salt, and water is a long one. As the mixture gurgles, you cut up the cucumbers, removing undesirable bumps and bruises. Then you put the little guys in a jar and pour the hot brine over the top of them. When sealed, the jar lid snaps tightly closed. On the outside of the jar is a white sticker which reads, "pickle." But if the seal was broken at that moment, the green thingamabobs wouldn't be pickles, they would be cucumbers. For a pickle to adequately develop to its full potential, it needs to stay in the brine.

When you come to Christ, you're labeled as Celestial. (Celestial means that you are capable of living comfortably with God because of the Atonement of Jesus Christ.) You are justified in saying that you have the potential to become so. And if justification is your label, then the pickle is the sanctification. You become what you're labeled when you remain with what you know is true. All of us are God's pickles. If we stay in the brine, we will become what we were originally destined to do (Daniel 12:3).

Now comes the definition of the two words that Elder Christofferson mentioned. Justification means to take away the sting of past mistakes, while sanctification changes your very nature. In simple terms, justification is your immeasurable potential to become celestial (1 Corinthians 6:11). Sanctification means that you are celestial (Romans 3:24). It becomes your identity. Eventually, we will be perfect through Jesus Christ, but only if we remain with Him. If you stray, come back. That's why He is also the Good Shepherd. The Lord loves stragglers.

How sad is it when people say that they aren't spiritual material? They open up their jar of pickles too soon, and of course, they're not going to taste like pickles. It's going to be a cucumber. When you open the jar, you break the seal. It's the power of our bond with the Savior that makes us celestial. When you open the pickle jar and try to put the lid back on, it's no longer sealed. It's the brine which changes a cucumber to a pickle, but it's the seal that prevents the outside contaminants from entering in. The seal comes from making promises with our Heavenly Father. The tighter the seal, the better the pickle. How can I change what I am inside? Stay immersed in it! Allow the seal to keep you immersed in it!! If you have already broken the seal between you and God in the past, that is where the previous chapter's topic comes in. Repent and come back. Let your journey begin again.

I'm not celestial yet, but that's ok, because someday I will be. I just need to stay in the gospel of Jesus Christ. Be immersed in the brine, and it will change you from who you are and what Jesus has imagined for you.

John 8:31 reads, "Then said Jesus to those Jews which believed on Him, If ye continue in my word, then are ye my disciples indeed."

Your justification can begin now. That was the purpose of my book. Discard the stickers the world is pasting across your spirit. They don't know what God has in store for you. You can become a pickle (metaphorically). You can become like Jesus Christ (1 Nephi 13:37). No matter how dark or scary your thoughts may be, this is your destiny, if you choose to stay.

Sources

1) Saints, President Russell M. NelsonPresident of The Church of Jesus Christ of Latter-day. "Christ Is Risen; Faith in Him Will Move Mountains." www.churchofjesuschrist.org, Apr. 2021, www.churchofjesuschrist.org/study/general-conference/2021/04/49nelson?lang=eng.

2) Ritter S. Monitoring and Maintenance of Brain Glucose Supply: Importance of Hindbrain Catecholamine Neurons in This Multifaceted Task. In: Harris RBS, editor. Appetite and Food Intake: Central Control. 2nd edition. Boca Raton (FL):

CRC Press/Taylor & Francis; 2017. Chapter 9. Available from: https://www.ncbi.nlm.nih.gov/books/NBK453140/ doi: 10.1201/9781315120171-9

3) Wiginton, K. (n.d.). *Signs you're mentally exhausted*. WebMD. https://www.webmd.com/mental-health/ss/slideshow-signs-youre-mentally-exhausted

4) Christofferson, D. Todd . "Justification and Sanctification." 2019, www.churchofjesuschrist.org/study/ensign/2001/06/justification-and-sanctification?lang=eng.

CHAPTER 6: RELIEF

You're clothed in priceless clothing during the anointing of a king. A priest comes forward with a jar of amber oil, which he pours reverently upon the head of one who has worked long and hard to arrive at this moment (Exodus 20:35). The atmosphere is perfectly still, one of awe, as this man receives the highest honor that he can receive, the divine right to rule (2 Samuel 12:7).

"It has been years in the making," Someone whispers.

"He has filled the measure of his creation." Another agrees.

As the crowned king rises, he turns to look at you, and your heart stops. You know him. He extends his hand to you, and you take it. Upon looking into a priceless oak mirror in front of you, you recognise that not only is this man a king, but you are his queen (Doctrine and Covenants 76:56, Isaiah 49:23). Brethren, bear with me and imagine the opposite scenario. I'm a woman, so this is my perspective on the story. They place crowns on your heads, which are made of perfectly cut glass. There you are, man and wife, having overcome the wiles and temptations of the evil one (2 Nephi 9:28). As you walk hand in hand onto a balcony overlooking hundreds of cheering faces below, you view the white-robed men and women, millions of them, likewise crowned with glory, waving and shedding tears of joy (1 Peter 5:4, Doctrine and Covenants 59:2).

Now, I do not know how it will be when Christ comes again, but I do know this: we all have the potential to inherit all that our Father has in store for us. To deny this would be to deny the purpose of our loving Heavenly Father.

Many people see the second coming of our Lord and Savior Jesus Christ as something to anticipate with dread (Revelation

1:7). The world sees our God as a harsh, unforgiving, immortal being who burns up mere mortals on a whim and coldly rules the Universe. Christ, on the other hand, is our loyal champion, our intercessor between us and the father (Mosiah 14:12, Romans 8:34).

Revelation is a demanding book for the mind to comprehend. It's the very last book of the bible, which many people call, "The Doomsday Chapters." I don't pretend to understand all that I read, but a particular verse in Revelation Chapter 7 struck a chord in my heart.

Chapter 7:9-10, 13-17 reads:

9 After this I beheld, and, lo, a great multitude, which no man could number, of all nations, and kindreds, and people, and tongues, stood before the throne, and before the Lamb, clothed with white robes, and palms in their hands;

10 And cried with a loud voice, saying, Salvation to our God which sitteth upon the throne, and unto the Lamb.

13 And one of the elders answered, saying unto me, What are these which are arrayed in white robes? and whence came they?

14 And I said unto him, Sir, thou knowest. And he said to me, These are they which came out of great tribulation, and have washed their robes, and made them white in the blood of the Lamb.

15 Therefore are they before the throne of God, and serve him day and night in his temple: and he that sitteth on the throne shall dwell among them.

16 They shall hunger no more, neither thirst any more; neither shall the sun light on them, nor any heat.

17 For the Lamb which is in the midst of the throne shall feed them, and shall lead them unto living fountains of waters: and God shall wipe away all tears from their eyes.

I'm a crier. For the longest time, it's been my means of coping (Exodus 2:23). Sometimes I sob uncontrollably, but I always feel a little better after I'm done (Psalm 88:1). When I came upon these verses, salty streams of water dribbled from my eyes onto my nose and my chin. In my heart, I knew that this battle would be worth it (2 Chronicles 20:15). All the days that I wondered if I would ever be healed of my toxic perfectionism or my debilitating anxiety were caught up in the arms of the Savior. As a mortal, my defects are never-ending, but when I thought of that scene, the Lord letting me be one of his followers, offering me a chance at liberation, my joy ran down my cheeks like a July rainstorm (Psalm 126:5). I know that Christ sees your affliction. For the final time, I repeat that I am not a doctor nor a psychologist but a humble servant of Christ. Take my words as you will. But I testify in the name of that Almighty God that He loves you as you were, are, and will be one day. Come to Christ, follow His commandments, and all will be made right in the end.

Activity:

After this instance of God rubbing away my tears, I realized how much of my time I spent complaining. It didn't matter what it was; I always seemed to find something to drag my feet about. Alma 37:37 says, "Counsel with the Lord in all thy doings, and he will direct thee for good; yea, when thou liest down at night lie down unto the Lord, that he may watch over you in your sleep; and when thou risest in the morning let thy heart be full of thanks unto God; and if ye do these things, ye shall be lifted up at the last day."

Maybe this is cliché, but if you're rolling your eyes at this, you're probably not doing it. In this activity, I invite you to start a gratitude journal. The easiest way to accomplish this in our technological age is to set a reminder on your phone. I invite you to find one thing you are thankful for every single day. Add an alarm on your phone that will remind you to search for the positive aspects. Some days might be better than others, and you will find many things to be grateful for. If you write it down somewhere, in a journal, on a sticky note, or on your phone, you are more likely to remember it. Gratitude is not a lost art (Doctrine & Covenants 46:32). It's a cord that further connects us to God. When I discarded the sarcastic cynicism from my life, I noted a gradual increase in my conviction towards my Savior and Father in Heaven. So, my invitation, as always, is to go try it for yourself. I promise this exercise will infuse your daily living with greater joy (1 Nephi 3:6). Resist the urge to grumble and show appreciation to the One who has given you so much.

Gratitude Challenge: Fill every line with something you're grateful for.

_____	_____	_____
_____	_____	_____
_____	_____	_____
_____	_____	_____
_____	_____	_____
_____	_____	_____
_____	_____	_____
_____	_____	_____
_____	_____	_____
_____	_____	_____
_____	_____	_____

_____   _____   _____
_____   _____   _____
_____   _____   _____
_____   _____   _____
_____   _____   _____
_____   _____   _____
_____   _____   _____
_____   _____   _____
_____   _____   _____
_____   _____   _____
_____   _____   _____
_____   _____   _____
_____   _____   _____
_____   _____   _____
_____   _____   _____
_____   _____   _____
_____   _____   _____
_____   _____   _____

***Note: as with many of the other techniques in this book, it's simple to forget to do some of these exercises as we become more occupied. That's ok. We're imperfect for a reason. If you notice yourself slipping back into the habit of whining about your neighbor, favorite sports team, or spouse, reroute yourself and start again. Remember that through Jesus Christ, we are able to make another go of it (Proverbs 28:13)

Courage

9/17/2024

Dear diary,

I know it's been a while since I've written, but I wanted to come back and make sure that my words were heard. I'm learning that life is a perpetual struggle (Alma 12:24). It's a balance between light and dark or good and evil, everything fighting for its place in life. However, there is an inherent virtue to it as well. I see it in so many different ways. Frederick Douglass said, "If there is no struggle, there is no progress." But I still wonder occasionally if I will be good enough for God because of my many flaws (1 Corinthians 2:3). My progress seems to be taking a *long time.*

How often have we asked ourselves, "Can I really do this? Am I good enough?" I personally have posed the question thousands of times. Is it a sign of faithlessness to do so? Are we giving in to the temptations of the Devil if we truly don't know if we have the capability to cross one more river, climb one more mountain? Am I truly going to be able to live with God someday?

Today, Nathan and I talked for a long time. We pondered about past mistakes and how they bleed into our current relationship (John 1:29). It's painful: the aftermath, like a hurricane ripping through our lives, and there's no doubt that there will be damage after certain events.

I used to cringe when I thought about the past: those horrible errors, the things I wish I could erase. I worried about committing the same blunder again, so my life became a frenzied hell vibrating between disgust about the past and dismay for the future.

On exploring an old diary the other day, I discovered that there were many pages that had been ripped out. It was the diary from when I first met my husband. At the beginning of our relationship, I was very uncertain, and I only chose to write when I was afraid or when I wondered if I was making the right decision. So, I ripped out those pages and threw them in the trash, destroying history. Now, I try to look back on my blunders with mercy. I miss those pages of my life, and now I wish that I hadn't belittled my own fallacies. "If only I had known," I tell myself, "Then I would have done something different."

Now, I don't want to. Learning to love your past is the key to accessing your future.

Golda Meir said, "One cannot and must not try to erase the past merely because it does not fit the present."

It is for this reason that I have come to the conclusion that the weakest people are often the bravest. Why? They have a past that may be ugly, but they trudge through the sleet and snow anyway, seeking to do that which is right (Ezra 10:4). Despite their doubts, these individuals continue in faith towards Christ, though sometimes they don't even know how. But they know where they're walking and why they're walking. Nothing impedes their steady course. Though we may not always be the best at what we wish to achieve, we can always be the most consistent.

Like me, you may be wondering if God would ever decide to lift you to his level if you would ever be even close to reaching His majesty. You can. You, and your mortal body, can be lifted up to see your Father in Heaven and your loved ones someday, through Jesus Christ. If you choose to follow Him now, Jesus Christ will bring you with Him. You can become celestially powerful. Your mental health struggles will not impede you from becoming great.

Activity: Balance

As you are nearing the end of this book, I know you may put it down and never think of it again. I can definitely admit that I've done it myself. With this activity, I wish for you to grasp the importance of divine balance in our lives. Negative thinking patterns don't vanish overnight. This could take months or years of your life to achieve. It's your constancy that matters. This will put your life into equilibrium.

It has been mentioned several times the tendency for our brains to blow small things out of proportion in our lives. This is a survival tactic taken to the extreme, our brains attempting to defend us from something that truly appears real. In this exercise, I ask you to be brave, and confront what your brain has concocted for you over the space of many years (Psalm 46:2).

Here's an example.

Ellen comes back from the testing center at her university. She just found out that she failed her final and will subsequently have a failing grade in the class. It's maddening to know how much time she dedicated just to lose her grade at the very end of the semester. For a while, Ellen fumes and stomps around her neighborhood, muttering unintelligible things about how her teacher did this and how now she's going to be behind on her major. Then, the sadness sets in. Shaky breaths puff off her lips, and she fights the sob welling up in her throat. Finally, Ellen sits on an icy park bench, shoving her hands into her pockets. A tear quietly slips out. Then, surrounded by snow and raw emotion, Ellen allows herself to reflect (3 Nephi 17:3). Her mind sifts through both the good and the bad.

She acknowledges these fleeting emotions with quiet meditation.

- That was a very difficult exam. There might have been other people who failed it as well.

- I'm hurting because I wanted to pass so badly.

- I'm angry because I studied so diligently, and I still didn't make the cut.

Ellen paused to stare at a red cardinal perched quietly on a pine tree. Though her emotions were strong, she continued to reason through them.

- I'm glad I took the class. I made some new friends and grew as a person.

- Sometimes, I fall short, but I can try again.

- This isn't the end. There are many options still waiting for me.

- What can I take from this experience?

Do you see the formula here? I call this the piercing-it-all-together experience. Ellen didn't tamp down her distress or ignore her feelings, but she didn't let them control her either. They came and went like the wind grazing a blade of grass. This is what I encourage you to do as well. Tie it all together. Allow yourself to process confusion, anger, hurt, pain, or worry, but don't let them stay at your house. There is always a sunny side to life (Alma 5:7). Find it. Let the yin and yang settle in your soul. I invite you to try this method for yourself. It takes practice, but I promise the results are worth it.

Our Love For God

In the year 2020, the world was ravaged by a worldwide pandemic. Our lives were rocked. Loved ones dropped like flies from varying symptoms, and there are many of us who lost those who are closest to us. Doors closed in every direction. People lost their jobs. Others lost their lives. Our hearts began to fail us (Doctrine and Covenants 88:91). Across the globe, we were all searching for the same four-letter word: hope. Did it truly exist for us? Would toilet paper, flour, or our trust in humanity ever return?

"Watch ye, stand fast in the faith, quit you like men, be strong. Let all your things be done with charity." -1 Corinthians 16:13-14

What is our hope for the future? How can we ever truly find happiness in a world that is so completely backward and sickeningly caught up in Satan's chains? We must know what we stand for. We must plant our feet on the path towards God and march onward courageously. For we fear not men, but it's our God that we fear.

God created you to succeed, to conquer, and to champion (1 Chronicles 28:20).

The topic of repentance, forgiveness, and remission is a continual process. Like constructing a house, it requires materials, labor, and occasional missteps. It's interesting how God remarked that He would let our sins slide, that He would forget they even happened. But what about us? Our misjudgments often sear themselves into our cranium like a brand, leaving a painful scar of what we delivered upon ourselves. My advice to you is: stop punishing yourself. Making yourself feel terrible for your past destroys your future. Just as we discussed in the Repentance chapter, your sins have already been forgiven. If you feel you don't know how to let go of your mistakes, ask God. I have a cure-all, fix-all method, but so many people refuse to use it because it seems so simple. Talk to your Heavenly Father. Ask Him to help you.

Surrender

I love it when the words "leap" and "surrender" are used. The imagery is fantastic. When I think of a leap, I think of a toddler jumping off the deep end into their parent's arms. How do they know they'll be caught? What awaits them if they're not? But they don't allow those thoughts to penetrate their minds. Children simply take the plunge. Surrender means to wave the white flag. It is to bestow every fiber of your soul or to unleash something that has long been stored inside. To surrender is to find your wings and fly.

I remember there was a time that we were all gathered as a family reading our scriptures, my four other siblings and I. We had recently touched the topic of trust upon reading Alma 36:3, which says, "And now, O my son Helaman behold, thou art in thy youth, and therefore, I beseech of thee that thou wilt hear my words and learn of me; for I do know that whosoever will put their trust in God shall be supported in their trials, and their troubles, and their affliction, and shall be lifted up in the last day."

We debated back and forth how much confidence someone must have, to be so completely and utterly enlisted in the cause of that great being. What did it mean to trust in the arm of the flesh versus the direction of God? My father looked directly at my youngest brother at the time, Max. Max was five years old and clearly not following the intellectual conversation very well.

"Max, if your friend told you to jump off of a cliff, would you do it?" My dad queried.

Max pondered for a second and replied, "No."

My dad continued, "If your sister asked you to jump off a cliff, would you do it?"

Max looked at me and easily responded, "No."

"Would you jump off of a cliff if I told you to do it?"

Max immediately began to cry, "Daddy, why would you ask me to jump off of a cliff?"

My dad felt pretty bad after that little exercise, but the principle is there. If my father would have asked, Max would have jumped, even if his little body quivered at the thought. There is a certain level of conviction that must be displayed within each of us, but not to our neighbor, grocer, nor our friendly policeman. No, this conviction varies for the souls surrounding us, but to our father, the response is unwavering. "Of course, I would follow thee."

Can we truly be afraid when we are in the hands of the Father, the architect of the universe? God will catch us every single time, without fail.

I learned this lesson when I took a trip to a mountain village in Mexico.

WHY SATAN USES FEAR

We often cannot see much further beyond the point that is directly ahead of us. That's how Satan desires that we lead our lives (1 Corinthians 7:5). Right here. Right now. A little pleasure here, some personal gratification there. We are living in the last days before the second coming of the Lord. In order for Satan to capture those powerful souls that Heavenly Father reserved for these current times, he has to be sneaky. It is easy to throw people off not in big, obvious ways but with something miniscule, like their perspective. Satan will give us everything up front, right from the get-go. But his contribution is fleeting and quickly diminishes in value with time. It is almost like a low-risk or high-risk stock investment. There are companies that fluctuate in their success, flowing up and down. Positive, negative, back and forth; it is a serious game of trust to place one's card with these organizations. Other companies, on the other hand, have established their trustworthiness. Their market value is consistent. Within reason, they are considered safe investments. God is a sure investment for our souls (2 Nephi 4:34). He is unshakeable. And He sent His son Jesus Christ to help us clean up the messiness of our lives. This messiness is what often causes us to lose eternal perspective. But

Jesus Christ is our broom. Eternity is so expansive that we can't even imagine the possibilities within our grasp! You are limitless.

This was my case when I joined my in-laws on a family trip to Mexico.

When I was a Junior in college, my husband invited me to visit his parents in Mexico. Nathan's parents were mission presidents for our church at the time and were very anxious to meet me. It was an amazing trip. We spent some time visiting members in the area and enjoyed the Latino hospitality, but one of the trip favorites was a series of crystal blue lakes called Tamasopo.

Disclaimer: I've never been cliff jumping before, nor have I cared to try, seeing how my stomach does backflips looking over the balcony of a second-story apartment. I entered Tamasopo believing we would be swimming and playing in the beautiful water, but much to my alarm, we rented eight life jackets and headed to the top of a small cave that rested twenty feet above the water. My gut clenched, and I squeezed my fists hard to prevent the panic from setting in. I really, really did not want to leap off that rock. Not that I was going to say anything because Nathan's nine-year-old nephew easily bounded off before me. I was going to die in the middle of a Mexican paradise. Well, at least I would perish somewhere magnificent. Maybe they could put on my headstone: killed by a heart attack on her way down to her doom. I liked it. I was going to die. Goodbye, cruel world. I counted to three, thirteen, then thirty, and I took the plunge. What a nosedive. I pondered all of my life decisions as I plummeted to my watery grave. Gravity quickly carried me down the steep fall, and I let out a tiny shriek before I slammed the water in my signature cannonball. Hmm, that wasn't so bad, actually. I pinched myself to make sure I hadn't passed into the spirit world. Nope, still alive. So I did it again. and again… and again. After a while, my stomach rolled a little less, and I felt a lot braver for doing it. Maybe I will enlist in the Olympics next for the ten-meter dive!! Actually, probably not.

To make a long story short, Satan wants you to flounder, falter, and, eventually, fail. He's been at it for thousands of years, cooking up creative methods to drag your soul carefully away from the truth (2 Nephi 28:21). Because God continues to send his most resilient spirits down to this earth, it's becoming harder and harder to tempt them to do the things that other generations did before them. Did you know that the word damn means to stop? Yep, but here on earth, Satan isn't completely able to damn you forever. That's what the Atonement of Jesus Christ is for. But one very effective method for Satan to cause you to stall for long periods of fear is to drive fear into your heart. Fear prevents you from moving forward. When you're afraid of heights, you freeze. You never vault off the high dive because your legs can't brave the climb of anticipation.

The moral of the story is that sometimes you just have to jump. I knew the water would catch me, but I worried about the rocks possibly lurking under the turquoise shadows. I promise you that Jesus Christ is going to catch you, regardless of your circumstances. You aren't going to die an ignominious death because God's plan is foolproof. However, the path may be slightly different for you than what you expected. There will be some high falls, and at times, you may question whether or not to let yourself drop (Doctrine and Covenants 11:12).

I say this with greater understanding than I have ever had at any other point in my short existence. You have one shot at this life. One chance. So live it. Choose God.

Courage

When I was in my first semester as a student at BYU Idaho, I attended an Old Testament class, where I was able to study the book of Exodus. In these chapters, the Hebrew's backs and spirits are broken by the oppressive bondage of slavery. Though the Egyptians still clearly had the upper hand with the Hebrews, the slave's numbers continued to swell at an alarming rate. The Egyptians were afraid. Rigorously, the taskmasters "made their lives bitter with hard bondage… in all manner of service" (Exodus 1:14). To the Egyptians' dismay, the harder they pushed the Hebrews, the more fruitful they became. Shiphrah and Puah were midwives among the Hebrew people. Despite their lowly states, they were summoned by the Pharaoh of Egypt. He commanded them that when they helped a woman birth a son, they were to kill him, but if it were a girl, they could let her live. At that moment, these two women had a decision to make. They were ordered by the king to do something that would be treason against their people and a sin against their God, but defiance of the Pharaoh certainly led to death. In Exodus 1:17, it says, "But the midwives feared God."

In the face of certain death, these two women clung to their dedication to God and disobeyed the order of their King. They delivered EVERY child born, male or female, and no doubt saved the lives of hundreds of Hebrew boys despite the danger apparent in their circumstances. Though they were afraid, though they were within the grasp of the jaws of death, these stoic women would not break. When brought before the king, they boldly declared, "Hebrew women are different from your women. We are strong. Our women gave birth to their babies before we could reach them, and they hid their baby boys away so we could not kill them."

God did not let Shiphrah and Puah fall. God delivered them from the wrath of Pharaoh and raised their houses to even greater heights. We will come to the point in our lives where we will be faced with the choice to serve God or to give in to the pressures of the world. Now, it is our turn to have courage. Though we may not be faced with the prospect of death or the bitterness of slavery, we are faced with chances to be courageous every day. When the time came for Shiphrah and Puah to choose, they didn't back down. Though the world may say otherwise, the same is applicable to us. When we are faced with a decision, we must ask ourselves, "Is my heart centered on God? Am I willing to lay down my own selfish desires and fall into the ranks of the armies of Zion?"

This is dedication; this is clinging to the word of the Lord as if one's very life depended on it because it did. They took the leap of faith. They chose Christ (Matthew 22:14). The days are coming when we will have to make choices, difficult ones, that will stretch us to our limits and cause us to either cling to God or push him away. Our challenge in these latter days will be to be courageous in our daily living and in the day-to-day decisions that will ultimately lead to our eternal destiny. Though the answer may be difficult, we can be assured that it will always, always be our God.

I invite you to keep fighting for your mental freedom from bondage. Don't let Satan's chains restrain you from becoming who you were meant to be.

Thoughts on Suicidal Thoughts and Deep Feelings

I've always believed there are few people in our lives who will ever reach the point of being our idols, the ones you always seem to call when nothing is going right. These are the ones who you strive to emulate because you know they are the caliber of person you always desired to be. That's my Aunt Carrie. I always saw my

Aunt Carrie as invincible, and I see her as even more so now… This is her story.

Anxiety melds into the spirit of young children and develops with them as they age. As a child, my Aunt Carrie was convinced that mountains would wash away her home or that trees would collapse on the house. Gusts of wind rattled her until her body stiffened from the mental paralysis. Hands over her head, the girl whimpered behind a red couch.

As she aged, Carrie converted from physical anxiety to spiritual anxiety. Instead of nightmares about the weather, the teenager grappled with extreme self-deprecation. When she was fourteen years old, thoughts of suicide and harming others oozed into Carrie's mind. In her own words, ***"The thoughts were so real that I was afraid that if I talked about it, it would happen.*** I worried I would kill myself or someone I loved. I felt like I didn't have control of myself. I was terrified I would drive off a bridge every day heading to school. I knew there were guns in my grandma's house, and I knew they were loaded."

Even after returning home from college, Carrie had to face that world again. It was a dark cloud, a tiny space where she could barely see. She took a deep breath, and the air rushed from her lungs. The space shrank even smaller. Creeks sounded from the murk, and Carrie's pulse roared in her ears. But she didn't call out. How could she? What would they say? What would they think of her? Because my aunt didn't know how to talk to anybody about it, she enveloped it in a charming smile. The room compressed in size.

It wasn't until Carrie had her first son, Jamison, that she vocalized what she was going through. In a final attempt to escape herself, she reached out to her sister-in-law, who finally convinced her to speak with a doctor.

In her own words, Carrie explained, "I was really good at masking my fear. I was a state FFA officer, and wearing that jacket was another mask for me. When I put it on, it helped me to feel powerful and confident, but it was a mask, just like a smile is a mask. I looked like everything is ok, but it wasn't."

Carrie found that there was a lot that she was hiding behind. Grandma's dusty couch, the jacket, and her smile protected her. Even once Carrie grasped how to utilize the Savior's love, the recovery didn't end there. When she accepted the Savior's Atonement, that cloud dissolved. The suffocating fear ceased. It was then that Heavenly Father could use Carrie for what she was meant to do. Her Bishop helped her to be honest and get things off her chest. For the first time in her life, she felt clean (2 Nephi 25:16). It took a while to learn how to smile for real because Carrie didn't know who she was. It all came down to figuring out it's ok to be vulnerable.

'Use the appropriate face for the appropriate expression for the appropriate emotion.'

Carrie's grandma used to always tell her that. When you're sad, be sad, when you're happy, be happy. Now Carrie says it how it is. When she smiles, she feels it. It's a lifelong process. Carrie is still adapting to being herself and being ok with it. Sometimes she still feels like a little kid hiding behind the couch, but then Carrie knows she has the Savior's sacrifice (Alma 34:10).

I have only seen my Aunt Carrie cry once. Her smile swaddles me in a bundle of love. I know she loves me. I know she's happy, but maybe not always. She has learned that hiding the fear only compounds the problem. It takes a lifetime to recognise who we truly are, but it is a life that does not need to be impeded by your mental health. Your fears do not determine your destiny. You do!

Hope is waiting for you. Look for it. It waits for you beyond the horizon. For so long, my aunt believed there was no one who could ever help her leave her depression.

Suicidal thoughts are real, and they're scary. As always, Satan is sneaky and may try to sneak in these emotions when your guard is down, or you are undergoing extreme stress. Pay attention to your statements to others and your personal ideas that enter your mind.

The scars we wear are not something to be disguised under long-sleeved shirts or shielded with thick sunglasses. Our Savior has His own scars (Doctrine and Covenants 6:37). Despite the gut-twisting torture Christ endured, He maintained the marks of the nails that pierced His perfect skin. We honor the scars of our Savior. He is not ashamed of his wounds, so why should you be?

Suicidal thoughts can range in severity and depth but are generally accompanied by desperation, reckless behavior, distance from loved ones, or severe mood swings. I want you to pay attention here. Jesus Christ and your family will not love you any less if you have ever had these thoughts (2 Thessalonians 2:16). In fact, in 2022, more than 22 million Americans had some form of suicidal thought (I will display common expressions below).[4] I've lost loved ones to suicide, and I, too, have felt a couple of these before. It is our body's reaction to a great loss or trauma, but it isn't the answer. Suicide is never the answer.

President Jeffrey R. Holland declared, "To any of our youth out there who are struggling, whatever your concerns or difficulties, death by suicide is manifestly not the answer. It will not relieve the pain you are feeling or that you think you are causing. In a world that so desperately needs all the light it can get, please do not minimize the eternal light God put in your soul before this world was. Talk to someone. Ask for help. Do not destroy a life that Christ gave His life to preserve. You can bear the struggles of this mortal life because we will help you bear them. You are stronger than you think. Help is available from others and especially from God. You are loved and valued, and needed. We need you! 'Fear not: believe only.'" [5]

Activity: Suicidal Thoughts

Below is a list of common suicidal thoughts. We have learned extensively throughout this book that your thoughts do not define you. They don't! It can be scary to recognize that you have thought these things before. If they are in your vocabulary, erase them. You may think that you are only joking right now, but when life hits you hard, Satan will use those phrases to attack your spirit harder than you ever thought possible. I draw these phrases from *The Depression Project*, an organization dedicated to aiding people through their depressive thoughts. [6]

1) I'm not enough

2) *All my friends and family hate me*

3) I will never overcome _____

4) I can't do anything right

5) I'm such a failure

6) *I'm a burden*

7) *Everyone would be better off without me*

8) *I can't do this anymore*

9) I wish I was more like him/her - they're so much better than me

10) *There's no point to any of this*

11) Nothing good I achieve will ever be noticed

12) I'm a terrible mother/father

13) *No one would notice if I just disappeared*

14) My friends all talk trash about me behind my back

15) I'm so ugly

16) Something bad always happens

17) My depression just brings everyone else down with me - I'm so selfish

18) *I don't deserve the love of anyone in my life*

19) *I can never make up for all the harm I've caused*

20) My parents must be so disappointed in me

21) I'm a loser who will never amount to anything

22) I'm no fun to be around

23) I should have said _____ - I'm such an idiot

24) *I'd rather be anyone else than me*

25) *Life is just a burden*

26) I'm such a drama queen - the smallest things always trigger me

27) *I bet my parents regret having me*

28) I'll never be enough for a romantic partner

29) If I died, no one would go to my funeral

30) The poor treatment I receive from others is all my fault

31) I'm not depressed; I'm just lazy

32) I'm such a weak person

33) If anyone really cared about me, they would be with me

34) I can't even clean my house - I must be completely useless

35) The world is so cruel and cold

36) People just tolerate me - they don't like me

37) I turn everyone in my life bad

38) I should be doing better in my life by now

39) I've squandered every good opportunity I've ever had.

40) I don't deserve to have my depression; people have it so much worse.

41) I cannot do things I know I'm capable of.

42) Anyone would hate me if they got to know me.

43) *I will die alone*.

44) I'm so pathetic that I can't even take my own life.

45) I don't deserve anything good to ever happen to me.

46) Everyone who likes me is lying to me.

47) No one will ever truly understand me.

48) I've never achieved anything.

49) No one wants to hear my opinion.

50) I'm worthless and unlovable.

Out of this list, I have put in italics anything that may be categorized as suicide ideation. Suicidal ideation generally leads to a plan or a desire to end one's life. These other thoughts are often building blocks for ideation. They erode self-love and create horrific despair. This is why I write this portion with three mentalities. One: you are noticing that your self-esteem is very low due to frequent usage of any of these phrases that are not in italics. Two: you frequently say or think of many of the sentences not in italics, as well as a couple that are in italics. Three: you may have noticed someone you know or love who utilizes a diversity of these expressions.

Group One:

Refer to the beginning of the book about your divine identity as well as other resources that teach about your value to God.

Safety Buddy- these people are of the highest trust value. If you haven't found someone who you can confide in now, take the leap. If you feel you can't confide this information, consider therapy or a trusted leader.

Talk to God about your value to Him. He will answer you, but He wants you to call out.

Group Two

**Safety Buddy- We need you here. We love you. Shame is a common tactic for Satan to trick you into hiding. Don't fall for it. If you are considering ending your life, or if you are having frightening thoughts of doing so, call your safety buddy immediately. (The suicide national hotline recommends you have at least three trusted people you can call in case of emergency.)

**Suicide Hotline: If you don't feel safe communicating with any of these people, call this number. You aren't a burden to them. You are God's precious child.

Call or text 988 to communicate with licensed individuals about your current situation.

**Before you take any action, get on your knees and pray to God for his help

Group Three

It's a mistaken notion that discussing suicide with someone who appears suicidal may cause them to actually commit the act. The opposite is actually true. I know it sounds scary to ask, but I promise that the guilt of losing a person is much worse than the pain of questioning. If you believe someone may be contemplating ending their life, simply ask them, "Are you thinking about suicide?" One of the most exhausting things about self-destructive thoughts is that the individual feels completely isolated. Often, they refuse to reach out for help in an obvious manner because they don't want to weigh down other people with their problems. Sometimes, they may feel that other people will judge them. This only increases loneliness.

Other signs of suicide (Mayo Clinic):[6]

- Getting the means to take your own life, such as buying a gun or stockpiling pills

- Withdrawing from social contact and wanting to be left alone

- Having mood swings, such as being emotionally high one day and deeply discouraged the next

- Being preoccupied with death, dying, or violence

- Increasing use of alcohol or drugs

- Changing normal routine, including eating or sleeping patterns

- Doing risky or self-destructive things, such as using drugs or driving recklessly

- Giving away belongings or getting affairs in order when there's no other logical explanation for doing this

- Saying goodbye to people as if they won't be seen again

- Developing personality changes or being severely anxious or agitated, particularly when experiencing some of the warning signs listed above

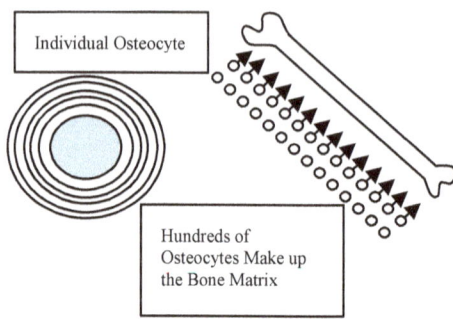

If you notice any of these other signs, ask God to give you the strength and courage to help this individual. If this person responds that they are considering taking their life, ask them if you can sit with them until they feel better. Listen to them if they are willing to talk. Ask them to call another loved one while you are in the vicinity with them. You could encourage them to call the suicide hotline. Do not leave them until you are certain of their condition. You could be the means of saving their life.

Building a Rock Solid Foundation

Have you ever wondered why it's so hard to break a bone? Obviously, with the right amount of force, anything can splinter, but for the most part, our bodies are fairly well protected. It all comes down to the molecular structure of the skeleton. Every single part of our anatomy is composed of cells. Many of these cells are fluid and soft. Bone cells (or osteocytes) begin this way, but over time, they harden and solidify. Much like a gobstopper, osteocytes begin with a single layer from a blast cell (the chewy center). The blast cell works like a construction crew. It builds up coatings around an osteocyte that strengthens the entire bone. Layer upon layer, the bone cell thickens until it is strong enough to join a matrix. A matrix is made of hundreds of bone cells, or osteocytes, which secure the durability of a bone.

Every day, you create micro-damages to your skeleton by walking, sitting, bouncing a basketball, etc. All of these things produce minuscule hairline fractures of bone. This is where the bone blast cells come back into play. Like Bob, the builder, they know they can fix the fragmentation. It's their job. That's also why we are able to heal quickly from a broken bone with a splint. The osteoblasts simply begin to rebuild again.

Of course, this process has been oversimplified to meet my point, but it is a powerful lesson regarding your spiritual development. Do not let little fractures cripple you.

You know who you are now. In this last chapter I wish to elaborate on the people you love. You may wonder at times if you are wounding the ones you love when you're trying to overcome your mental health struggles. You may worry occasionally that something will happen to those you love: a friend, spouse, or child.

I'd like to suggest a couple of ways that you can rebuild self-inflicted fractures. If you want to prevent your bones from breaking, you drink milk, you eat spinach, or you take a calcium supplement. Worry is a clash of mind and matter. It diminishes the zest of life and turns hairline fractures into terrible ruptures. We've discussed over and over the need to combat severed thoughts, so now is the time to begin.

When you are crazed with panic over the well-being of your loved ones, know that these are splinters in your well-being. But you can fix them. Regardless of all your best efforts, the lives of your loved ones will always be slightly out of your hands. When your subconscious burns with degrading ideas of self-harm, turn to these methods.

Here are some small modifications to your thoughts that may assist you in feeling lasting relief.

1) Write down the spiritual experiences in your life. If you aren't much of a journalist, at least invest time in that. Your spiritual foundation will be fortified when you are feeling the pressure more intensely.

2) Immerse yourself in the scriptures. Even sometimes, when we are faithful students of the scriptures, we're not diving into the meaning nor asking God to help us understand. Dig deep. No matter how long you read, plead with God to give more meaning to your life through these passages.

3) Pray every single day. Prayer is the gateway to heaven (2 Chronicles 7:14). As with scripture study, it isn't the length of the prayer that matters, but the soul of the prayer. Lift your heart up to God in heartfelt prayer. He will always answer.

***Note: There is nothing wrong with turning to therapy, medication, or other forms of mental health aids if you are drowning. As mentioned at the beginning of this book, this is simply another resource to help you shift your thinking. Please do not fall into the trap of ignorance. There are trained medical professionals to whom God has provided experience and empathy. Don't hesitate to turn to these methods if you feel you must do so. There's no shame in asking for help.

New Beginnings and Hard Goodbyes

I tiptoed a cracked sidewalk, the yellowing cottonwood trees shivering at my entrance into their world. It's fall again. Another year was fading into a tranquil state of rest. Tufts of winter wheat reached for my hands, and I let my fingertips rustle through them. Students returned to the hustle and bustle of homework and college parties. But I remained there. My spirit connected with the trees as hundreds of their leaves twirled to the ground in front of me.

I'm a new person since I began to write this book nearly one year ago. I'm more considerate of my failures and more accepting of my anxiety. This fall I entered the nursing program; my dream came true! There was just one problem: the design wasn't mine. The first week I floundered under the sheer weight of information. I really did not like nursing at that point.

I couldn't do it. It was too much, so I returned to the trees. I've always considered them my friends, their sloping boughs reaching down to offer me consolation. Remember that fear is Satan's greatest trick. Life doesn't get any easier. It just doesn't. But I've found ways to ground myself. Just like I turn to the trees for my refuge, you can go to Christ again and again. Meditate again and again. Repent again and again. It is a never-ending cycle that ends with you always being in the Savior's arms.

Throughout my entire life, I've struggled with feelings of self-worth, but I only ever seemed to end with my thousands of inadequacies. I'm too short. I'm not pretty. I'm not fast enough. I will never be smart enough.

Where do these perpetual thoughts stem from? Who plots in every moment to destroy our souls? You guessed it. The enemy himself. The son of the morning, long fallen and eternally immersed in the pitch black.

My hope stems from Christ's never-failing invitation to "come."

You are a child of a Heavenly Father who knows and loves you. He sent you here at this place and at this time to learn how to succeed. Learn is the keyword here. We are always learning, whether we want to or not! Our brains are hardwired to do so; call it evolution or divine inspiration, but you can overcome your fears. Work as hard as you possibly can. Give it your best shot! But remember that if you try to do it without God, you'll never achieve anything worthwhile. Some of the most successful people in this world are still miserable. They are lacking something, and I would argue that it's a relationship with a loving Heavenly Father. As you put in the time and strive to develop a real understanding of who God is, you will come to see that perhaps you do have the capacity to do all of those crazy dreams that are locked in your heart. You can overcome your negative thinking patterns one by one.

This is the process of recognising, shaping, and erasing. My dearest wish is that this book changed you in some way, even if it was a micro-adjustment. As words of parting, I would like to share this poem, written by our favorite new gadget, AI.

Rise above the storm, like a growing tree,

Roots in the present, branches wild and free.

In the canvas of chaos, paint serenity's hue,

A masterpiece of healing, resilience anew.

The sun may set, and shadows may play,

But within, a light will guide the way.

Fear may knock, but courage answers the door,

Anxiety defeated, strength evermore.

Let the verses of overcoming sing,

In the heart's cathedral, hope takes wing.

For beyond the shadows, a brighter morn,

A testament to the strength reborn.

ACKNOWLEDGEMENTS

Oh, what a journey this has been! For me, creating a book has always been a distant dream, but now it's a reality. I would like to thank my husband, Nathan, first and foremost, for believing in me every step of this voyage. He is the one who kept me on track and has reminded me over and over that I am enough for Jesus Christ.

My wonderful editing team has taught me a world of knowledge regarding publishing and editing. Thank you, Carl, Billy, and Skai, for being so patient with me and being willing to instruct such a new author through the process.

There are many personal stories written throughout this book. Thank you to every individual who has contributed a piece of their life to this book. You are very loved.

Finally, I would like to thank my God and Savior for inspiring me with words to write and hearts to lift. My husband once observed that this book was greatly inspired by the words of the Holy Ghost. I know that to be true.

It is liberating to know that this is my small contribution to the kingdom of God. Thank you all for reading. You are wonderful. Your story matters.

-Emree Webb

Sources

1) Benner, Jeff A. "Hebrew Word Definition: Messiah | AHRC." *Www.ancient-Hebrew.org*, 1999, www.ancient-hebrew.org/definition/messiah.htm.

2) Jennifer, Shannon. ""Just Checking" on the Ones We Love." *Adaa.org*, Anxiety and Depression Association of America, 7 Mar. 2019, adaa.org/learn-from-us/from-the-experts/blog-posts/consumer/just-checking-ones-we-love#:~:text=Intolerance%20of%20 uncertainty%20and%20jerry. Accessed 16 Sept. 2024.

3) https://www.psychologytoday.com/us/blog/the-savvy-psychologist/202105/how-cope-the-fear-loved-one-dying Marriott, Suzie, and Brittain Mahaffey. "Are Suicidal Thoughts Common? | Stony Brook Medicine." *www.stonybrookmedicine.edu*, 2022, www.stonybrookmedicine.edu/patientcare/askexpert/suicidalt houghts/marriott/mahaffey.

4) Apostles, Elder Jeffrey R. Holland Of the Quorum of the Twelve. "Fear Not: Believe Only!" *www.churchofjesuschrist.org*, Church of Jesus Christ of Latter Day Saints, Apr. 2022,www.churchofjesuschrist.org/study/general-conference/2022/04/23holland?lang=eng#p26.

5) The Depression Project. "50 Examples of Negative Thoughts When You Have Depression." *The Depression Project*, The Depression Project, 12 Feb. 2023, thedepressionproject.com/blogs/news/50-examples-of-negative-thoughts-when-you-have-depression?srsltid=AfmBOopw6MNblRhSGUfImukorIbd-CTMLxHZlJURYyS5wNIxwl7g3bOT. Accessed 22 Sept. 2024.